Instructor's Manual

Mark R. Bandsuch, *S.J.*
John Carroll University

James C. Swindal
John Carroll University

ETHICS and the CONDUCT of BUSINESS

Third Edition

John R. Boatright
Loyola University Chicago

PRENTICE HALL, *Upper Saddle River, New Jersey 07458*

©2000 by PRENTICE-HALL, INC.
Upper Saddle River, New Jersey 07458

ISBN 0-13-040073-4

Printed in the United States of America

TABLE OF CONTENTS

FOREWORD

This Instructor's Manual is a supplement to the third edition of *Ethics and the Conduct of Business*. Its purpose is to ease the task of preparing for classes and to provide ideas for interesting and productive classroom discussions. An instructor's manual is a resource that is most appreciated, perhaps, when time is short and the demands of teaching great. However, even the most experienced teachers are continually alert for new ideas and materials. The field of business ethics is constantly changing, and our courses must change with the times. It is my hope that this manual will serve not only as an aid for instructors but also as a spur to the development of the subject.

In the Foreword to the Instructor's Manual to the second edition of *Ethics and the Conduct of Business*, I acknowledged that the impetus for this project came from two of my former colleagues at John Carroll University, Mark Bandsuch and James Swindal, who developed many creative ideas for teaching business ethics that they wanted to share with others. I expressed my appreciation for their great dedication to the project and for their tremendous energies and abilities. I also acknowledged the valuable assistance of Cathleen Cunningham for her editorial skills.

In the preparation of the Instructor's Manual for the third edition, I have taken responsibility for updating the portions that have been affected by changes. The differences between the second and third editions of the book, which are summarized in the Preface to the third edition, are mainly in the first and last two chapters. For the third edition, I have also combined two previous chapters on marketing, advertising, and product safety into one chapter, with the result that the third edition contains fourteen instead of fifteen chapters. Eight new cases were written for the third edition, including cases on Texaco, Sears Auto Centers, and Shell Oil in Nigeria.

I encourage all users of *Ethics and the Conduct of Business*, 3rd edition, and this manual to contribute to the next edition of both works. Innovative teaching strategies are especially invited. Your active involvement in developing the field of business ethics will be most gratefully appreciated and acknowledged. Send all comments, suggestions, and other contributions to:

John R. Boatright
Department of Management
School of Business Administration
Loyola University Chicago
820 N. Michigan Avenue
Chicago, IL 60611
Internet: jboatri@luc.edu

As a further aid to instructors using *Ethics and the Conduct of Business*, 3rd ed., the publisher Prentice Hall has developed a website that includes teaching resources, test questions, case study questions, key concepts, Web destinations, and net search terms. The site address is: www.prenhall.com/boatright.

John R. Boatright
Loyola University Chicago

CHAPTER ONE

ETHICS IN THE WORLD OF BUSINESS

CHAPTER SUMMARY

Business ethics inquires into and justifies the decision-making process concerning what is right and wrong in all areas of business practice. The decision-making process occurs on the individual, organizational, and business system levels. This chapter explains how business decisions are made from the moral, legal, and economic points of view. The strengths and weaknesses of each perspective are reviewed before presenting an integrated approach that applies all three points of view in the business decision-making process. The chapter further discusses the relation between business ethics and economic, and between business ethics and the law, as well as the place of ethics in management. Finally, the distinction between morality (as a society's view of behavior that is right or wrong) and ethics (as the philosophical study of morality) is explained as a basis for the analysis and resolution of numerous issues in the business world through the application of ethical theories.

CHAPTER OVERVIEW

Introduction

Ethical issues arise in relationships with every corporate constituency, including employees, customers, suppliers, shareholders, and society at large. Rules of right conduct that are utilized in everyday life do not always resolve business questions, and problems arise when ethical considerations conflict with practical business concerns. Each role in a business organization involves unique responsibilities (such as the obligations of an employee to an employer or the fiduciary duties of management to the shareholders) that determine what a person should do. Business activity includes two features that limit the applicability of ordinary ethical perspectives, namely its economic characteristics and the fact that it takes place in organizations.

Business activity has a distinctive economic character. Business activity is concerned with economic relationships between parties, such as buyers and sellers and employers and employees. Employment relationships involve distinctive rights and duties, so that ethics in business is partly the ethics of economic relations.

Business activity takes place in large, impersonal organizations. Organizations are hierarchical systems of functionally defined positions that are designed to achieve particular goals. People occupying positions in organizations assume responsibilities that must be balanced with those of everyday life.

Levels of Ethical Decision Making

Decision making occurs on the *individual*, *organizational*, and *business system* levels. At the individual level, a person decides what he or she will do. At the organizational level, decisions involve an individual acting within his or her organizational role and are often expressed in procedures and policies, whereas the business system level involves systemic problems that concern industry practices and the economic system. These systemic problems require systemic solutions, such as an industry-wide code of ethics, government regulation or economic reform. Ethical displacement (addressing a problem on a level other than the one on which it appears) is often needed to resolve an ethical problem.

The Moral Point of View

Business decisions can be made from the moral, economic, and legal points of view. An integrated approach to business decision making combines all three points of view. Four morally relevant reasons for acting one way rather than another that constitute forms of *justification* are:

1. Considering the benefit and harm to all of the different parties involved.
2. Respecting the essential humanity of others.
3. Treating others with equality, fairness, and justice.
4. Caring for other persons in ways that nurture relationships.

The moral point of view uses *reason* or logic, not just feeling or conventional views, to justify decisions. And it requires *impartiality*, meaning that the interests of everyone, including one's self, should be given equal weight. Morality by its nature is public in the sense that it is a shared set of rules that are intended to be followed by everyone. A test of the moral point of view is, would you feel comfortable if colleagues, friends, and family knew about your decision, or if it were reported on TV or in the newspapers?

Criticisms of the moral point of view. People discount or disregard the moral aspect of business, arguing that the overriding consideration in business is profit maximization and efficiency as expressed in the economic point of view. The legal perspective must also be considered, but this approach is seen as a constraint on the economic position. Business, some contend, is *a*moral, which is not to say that business is *im*moral but only that morality is not relevant to business. Business has its own rules. Albert Carr argues that ethical conduct in business is merely *strategic behavior* within the rules that government has set. Business strategy aims solely at profits, but businesses preserve amicable relations and avoid dangerous hostilities with employees and other groups out of a strategic concern for long-term profits.

First, the moral point of view is essential, in combination with the legal and economic views, for the business decision-making process. A premise of the book is that business already utilizes the moral perspective to a significant degree. Second, strategic behavior without ethics may be impractical or even impossible to achieve because companies occasionally act non-strategically in the short run in order to receive the long-term strategic benefits of ethical action. One view holds that acting morally will ultimately provide greater long-term benefits to the business.

An Integrated Approach

Boatright suggests that the decision-making process in business should include the moral, economic, and legal points of view. The tension among the three points can often be resolved not through a tradeoff but through an ethically defensible decision that also satisfies a company's legal obligations and the economic demands of business. Business ethics attempts to think clearly and deeply about ethical issues in business and to arrive at conclusions that are supported by the strongest possible arguments. Philosophical ethics provides a set of concepts and theories that form an essential foundation for the discussion and resolution of specific ethical issues in business.

Ethics and Economics

Economics teaches that businesses should operate with only *profit* in mind. According to economic theory, firms in a free market utilize scarce resources or factors of production (labor, raw materials, and capital) in order to produce an output of goods and services, the demand for which is determined by the preferences of individual consumers who are trying to maximize their own satisfaction. Businesses try to increase production so that they receive from the sale of goods and services an amount equal to that spent on materials, labor, and capital (marginal revenues = marginal costs) and thereby achieve economic efficiency (maximum output for minimum input). On this view, business decisions *are* made and *ought to be* made purely on economic grounds, and ethics appears to have no place in business decision making.

Counterpoints. The economic perspective cannot stand alone as the basis for business decision-making for five reasons.

1. *The market system itself has an ethical justification.* Adam Smith's "invisible hand" argument for a free market depends on the assumption that a system of exchange based on self-interest will promote the public welfare. Thus, profit is not the ultimate *end* of business decision making but only a *means* for achieving a greater good. Furthermore, the invisible hand argument only justifies the pursuit of profit in *exchange;* it does not address ethical issues in *production* or *distribution*.
2. *Ethics is required by the market system.* The theory underlying the economic point of view already contains some ethical requirements, such as prohibitions against theft, fraud, insider trading, conflict of interest, and misappropriation of trade secrets. The economic theory also assumes perfect competition and the internalization of costs, which are seldom the case. These conditions are described by Milton Friedman as the "rules of the game," with which businesses are expected to comply in the pursuit of profit.
3. *The "rules of the game" cannot be set by government alone.* The economic arguments generally assumes that the "rules of the game" are set by outside forces, most notably government. However, it is unrealistic to expect that these forces are sufficient to set the "rules of the game," in which case businesses should perhaps be expected to exercise some form of self-regulation.
4. *Ethics influences economic behavior.* Studies of economic behavior show that individuals and firms do not act solely as rational utility maximizers but make decisions on the basis of such factors as a reputation for trust and a sense of fairness. This is illustrated in the case on Home Depot (Case 1.3).
5. *Public policy utilizes noneconomic values.* Business decision making takes place within a framework of public policy, which is guided, in part, by ethical values, such as fairness. For

example, a decision by a company such as Nike to contract with a supplier in Indonesia cannot be purely economic; it must also consider possible charges of human rights violations and other objectionable practices.

Ethics and the Law

Business decisions must also include the legal point of view because the law is a significant influence on business activity. Some argue that law is the only moral standard necessary to follow. (If it's legal, then it's morally okay.) This position is supported by two schools of thought: (1) that ethics is a matter of personal conduct, whereas law applies to public matters like business, and (2) that all unethical conduct in business has already been addressed by the law.

Why the law is not enough. Both of these schools of thought are mistaken. Ethics applies not only to public matters but also shapes the law. Furthermore, although much that is unethical in business is also illegal, the law cannot be a complete guide to ethical business practice for many reasons. Among these reasons are the following:

1. *The law is inappropriate for regulating certain aspects of business activity.* Certain behavior is immoral but not illegal because legislatures and courts are reluctant to intervene in ordinary business decisions unless significant rights or interests are at stake.
2. *The law is slow and needs time to develop.* The law develops in reaction to events and takes a long time to respond, so that problems can cause much damage before they are effectively addressed. Meanwhile, businesses have more information regarding their products and are thus able to anticipate problems and react much more quickly.
3. *The law includes moral concepts that are not precisely defined.* The legal point of view naturally overlaps with the moral point of view because the law uses general moral concepts, such as good faith and fiduciary duty, whose application is often a matter of time, place, and circumstance.
4. *The law is unsettled and is not always applied literally.* When the law is unsettled, the courts often use moral considerations to decide cases, and the courts may also refuse to interpret the law literally in order to avoid an immoral result. In appealing to morality, the courts are not substituting morality for law but are expressing the morality embodied in the law.
5. *The law is inefficient.* Businesses that emphasize the legal point of view often invite legislation and litigation where self-regulation could be more efficient.

Ethics and Management

Ethics in management is not merely applying the ethics of everyday life to business situations because situations in business are often different from those in everyday life. In addition, the task of a manager is not merely deciding what is right and wrong but also implementing ethics in business situations. The former can be described as *ethical management*, that is acting ethically as a manager, and the latter as the *management of ethics*, that is managing effectively in situations that have an ethical aspect. Both of these tasks require that a manager have certain knowledge and skills.

Furthermore, ethics in management is different because many of the rights and obligations of managers arise from occupying a particular *role*. Many roles, such as that of a purchasing agent, are precisely defined. However, the role of high-level management in leading an organization is open to debate. This role is variously described as: (1) an economic actor, (2) a trustee of resources, and (3) a quasi-public servant.

Morality, Ethics, and Ethical Theory

Moral (from the Latin *moralitas*) and *ethical* (from the Greek *ethikos*) have essentially the same meaning: a description of human behavior as right or wrong, good or bad that may be used interchangeably. However, subtle differences exist between *morality* and *ethics*. *Morality* is the sociological phenomenon of the existence of rules and standards of conduct in society that serve as the basis for mutually beneficial interaction. However, standards of *prudence*, such as looking both ways before crossing the street, and *etiquette*, such as not eating peas with a knife, are considered non-moral rules. In addition, moralities tend to be specific to societies, existing only at certain times and places. Moralities also include a complex vocabulary and pattern of reasoning for the purpose of evaluating the actions and practices of individuals, institutions, and society.

Ethics or moral philosophy is the philosophical study of morality. Ethics is a traditional area of philosophical inquiry along with logic, epistemology, and metaphysics. It can be either *descriptive*, which is an empirical inquiry into the rules or standards of a particular group, or it can be *normative*, which uses reasoning or arguments to justify the rightness of a morality. In another sense of the word, ethics consists of the rules and norms for specific kinds of conduct, such as the ethics of stockbrokers or the code of ethics for accountants. *Justification*, or the determination of right and wrong, has been challenged by two theses, namely cultural relativism and ethical relativism, which deny the possibility of justification.

Cultural relativism asserts that morality varies from one culture to another, since similar practices are regarded as right in some cultures and wrong in others. However, regarding practices as right or wrong does not necessarily make them so, nor does it exclude the possibility of demonstrating that moral beliefs are mistaken. For this reason, cultural relativism does not prohibit the possibility of justification. *Ethical relativism*, on the other hand, makes the philosophical assertion that there is no standard of right or wrong apart from the morality of a culture. Whatever practice a culture holds to be right is actually right for that culture. There is no possibility for justification because there exists no standard outside that culture. Ethical relativism results in an uncritical acceptance of all moral beliefs as equally valid.

CASE SUMMARIES

Case 1.1 Johnson & Johnson: The Tylenol Crisis

Johnson & Johnson had manufactured Extra-Strength Tylenol in capsule and tablet form since 1959. Tylenol became one of Johnson & Johnson's most successful products, accounting for 17 percent of the company's profits. Extra-Strength Tylenol constituted 70 percent of all Tylenol sales. Johnson & Johnson also enjoyed a tremendous amount of trust and goodwill from the public, nurtured in part by its adherence to the company credo of responsibility to customers, employees, shareholders, and the community. In 1982, seven people in the Chicago area died after taking Extra-Strength Tylenol capsules that were laced with cyanide.

Discussion Questions

1. How would you advise the CEO of Johnson & Johnson to respond to this crisis? What specific questions need to be addressed in formulating a response?
2. Should the product have been recalled? What are the arguments for and against a recall?
3. Ask students to analyze the question of recalling the product from the economic, legal, and moral points of view. Do the results differ from the decision that Johnson & Johnson eventually made?
4. What benefit did Johnson & Johnson derive from the company's credo? Could any other company with such a credo respond in the same way? Did the credo enable Johnson & Johnson to save the Tylenol brand, which many marketing experts thought was doomed?
5. Should Johnson & Johnson have continued to market Extra-Strength Tylenol in capsule form but with tamper-resistant packaging? What should Johnson & Johnson do upon discovering that a similar incident caused another death three years later?

Case Objectives

This case illustrates the possibility of an integrated approach to business decision-making. The obvious tensions between the different views should be addressed while acknowledging that they can be balanced and reconciled satisfactorily through the integrated approach. In retrospect, Johnson & Johnson made a sound (economic) business decision in recalling the product, but the case for the recall was not easy to make at the time. Arguably, the company's commitment to ethics enabled its executives to make the tough decisions, and the credibility of that commitment to employees and consumers contributed to the success of those decisions. The case shows the value of trust as a corporate asset. Johnson & Johnson's response to the Tylenol crisis has been described in many cases, including a Harvard Business School case "James E. Burke: A Career in American Business (A)" [case 5-390-015]; a video with the same title of an interview with James E. Burke, accompanied by company and media footage, is also available from Harvard Business School.

Case 1.2 Four Business Decisions

1. A sales representative for a struggling computer supply firm has the opportunity to close a multi-million dollar deal. The first delivery of machines will be on time but the subsequent deliveries may be delayed. Any delay in converting to the new system would be costly to the customer.
2. The director of research in an aerospace firm promotes a woman to head an engineering team based upon her superior knowledge of the project. Quick completion of the design and building of prototypes is vital to the success of the company. The men under her direction are subtly sabotaging the team's work due to their reluctance to work for a woman.
3. The vice-president of marketing for a major brewing company is concerned with her competitor's promotion of drinking on college campuses. College students account for a large percentage of beer sales and form lifelong loyalties to particular brands of beer. Underage drinking and alcohol abuse are major problems on college campuses.
4. The CEO of a mid-sized kitchen appliance firm is asked to merge with a larger company. The CEO will receive a substantial severance package and shareholders will receive a premium on their stock. However, the merger will result in the closing of a plant in a small town.

Discussion Questions

1. Should the sales representative close the deal without advising the customer of the problem? Exactly what should he say to the customer?

2. Should the director of research remove the woman from the head of the engineering team? What are his other alternatives? Which should he adopt?

3. Should the marketing executive go along with the competition and advertise aggressively to college students? Should she consider her own sense of right and wrong in making the decision?

4. Should the CEO recommend the merger? Should he consider his own interest or only those of the shareholders? Does he have any obligation (or right) to consider the interests of workers and the community?

5. What other facts would be helpful to know in each case? Why would these facts be relevant?

6. Whose interests are affected in each case? How does a decision maker decide which interests ought to be considered and how they should be weighted?

7. What are the consequences (both good and bad) of the different decisions? Are there any differences between short-term and long-term consequences? Which are more important?

8. Does the decision maker have an obligation or duty to any person or group? If yes, what are these? Are anyone's rights violated? If so, what are these rights? Do considerations of fairness or justice come into play in any of these cases?

9. What are the different points of view from which to approach each case? Can these views be integrated, and if so, how?

Case Objectives

These brief cases exemplify the types of ethical issues that can arise for managers and illustrate the idea of role morality. In each case, a manager faces a question of what to do in his or her role as a manager with a distinct set of responsibilities. The cases also offer a realistic view of the business decision-making process and an opportunity to apply the distinctions between the economic, legal, and moral points of view. In addition, they provide an introduction to the case study method (which will be the first introduction for some students), so that the instructor's handling of these cases may set the stage for all subsequent case discussions.

Case 1.3 The Ethics of Hardball

Toys "R" Us: Fair or Foul?

Employees of Toys "R" Us allegedly purchased $1.5 million worth of products from a lower-priced competitor, Child World, which was offering free gift certificates with major purchases. Toys "R" Us resold the Child World products, purchased at close to cost, for a profit and then used the $375,000 worth of Child World gift certificates to purchase additional products. This practice is apparently legal.

Discussion Questions

1. Should there be a law prohibiting this practice? Why may the law be inadequate to address this kind of competitive behavior?

2. Should the law be the sole guide to deciding whether actions such as the above should be done? What else should the managers of Toy's "R" Us consider in their decision to employ this practice?
3. Did Child World get what it deserved? That is, did its own conduct invite this kind of retaliation by competing so aggressively on price?

Case Objectives

The case brings out the strengths and weaknesses of using the law as a moral guide to business decisions. It also invites questions about the importance of the "moral tone" of competition in an industry and the responsibility of each company in an industry for setting this tone. Students may have never considered the idea that companies have obligations to their competitors.

Home Depot: Good Ethics or Shrewd Business?

In the wake of Hurricane Andrew in 1992, individual price-gougers were selling building materials at wildly inflated prices, but not Home Depot. Following the hurricane, the store continued to sell plywood at pre-hurricane prices. Even when plywood wholesale prices increased by 28 percent, Home Depot announced that it would sell plywood, roofing materials, and plastic sheeting at cost and take no profit. Home Depot negotiated with its suppliers to reduce prices to pre-hurricane levels in order to enable the store to maintain its retail prices.

Discussion Questions

1. Was Home Depot's behavior an act of good ethics or simply shrewd business? Imagine how an executive would argue in a meeting for the actions that the company took? What objections might other executives raise?
2. If the students have studied economics, ask them how the case might be discussed in an economics classroom. Present them with the evidence [cited in a footnote] of economic theorists who stress the importance of consumers' perceptions of fairness in their purchasing decisions.
3. Would it make any difference in this case whether a decision maker takes a short-term or long-term view? Which view should the decision maker take?
4. Does Home Depot (or any other business) have a responsibility to help the citizens hurt by the hurricane? Whose responsibility is hurricane relief?

Case Objectives

The main aim is to assess basic economic principles and determine how they apply in business decisions. The relationship between the profit-seeking of the economic point of view and the ethics of the moral point of view is complex in this case because consumers' economic behavior may be influenced by their perceptions of right and wrong. The case also provides an opportunity to introduce the concept of corporate social responsibility and the four criteria (urgency, proximity, capability, and need) that are covered in Chapter 14.

Case 1.4 A Sticky Situation

Kent Graham is an account manager for Dura-Stick Label Products, a company that specializes in labels for the automotive and appliance industries. Graham, who has a wife and two children, is concerned about losing his job because his performance at Dura-Stick has been mediocre. Graham is given an opportunity to land a big account with a present client, Spray-On Inc. The account requires the production of a label with a seven-color design and very precise graphics, which differs from the industrial two-color labels that Dura-Stick currently provides to Spray-On. Graham assured Spray-On that Dura-Stick could handle the label (although Dura-Stick had never produced anything but two-color labels). Graham gave a proposal to Spray-On knowing that the production of the labels would have to be contracted out and that Spray-On's interest in Dura-Stick was based primarily on its respect for the company's manufacturing capabilities. When the proposal was accepted, Graham had to decide what to say to Spray-On.

Discussion Questions

1. What should Graham say to Spray-On now? If you were Graham's superior, what would you want him to do? Is there any reason why the perspectives of Graham and his boss should differ?
2. What persons and groups are affected by Graham's decision? What are the specific benefits and harms to each? Should Graham be more concerned with his job and his family, his company, or his customers?
3. Has Graham actually lied to Dura-Stick? Would you say that, so far, Graham has acted dishonestly or merely thoughtlessly? Would he be lying if he continued to remain silent?
4. If you held Graham's job, is there anything that you would have done differently?

Case Objectives

This case shows that some ethical situations are more complicated than others and that they often develop from a series of seemingly inconsequential decisions. It could be argued that Graham has been more thoughtless than dishonest by allowing a misunderstanding to develop over time, so in the end no solution is wholly satisfactory. The case also provides an opportunity to discuss the complexities of truth-telling, in which keeping silent can be to lie and questions can arise over what one has an obligation to reveal.

Case 1.5 Argus Incorporated: A Leasing Triangle

Susan Solomon and Craig Dunston at Argus, Incorporated had failed to note that the lease for computer equipment from TekUSA had been assigned to an investor, Mr. Hayes. As a result, payments on the lease were sent to the wrong party, namely TekUSA, and a termination of the lease had similarly been negotiated with the same wrong party. Susan and Craig discover that they could perhaps avoid responsibility for their error by denying that they had ever received the Notice of Assignment and by destroying the document. Susan considers a "win-win" alternative that might satisfy all of the parties without engaging in any dishonesty.

Discussion Questions

1. Would not destroying the Notice of Assignment and denying that they had received it be a good business decision for Susan and Craig? After all, part of the responsibility lies with TekUSA, which did not catch the error. Even worse, TekUSA may have been aware of the error, in which case the company operated in bad faith by accepting payments and negotiating the termination. Although TekUSA may bear some responsibility, the company is a valuable supplier in trouble, and punishing it would also harm Argus. Mr. Hayes, too, bears some responsibility by not detecting the missed payments and notifying Argus earlier. In addition, Mr. Hayes might be unreasonable in his demands for a settlement.

2. Is it possible to develop a "win-win" solution that would satisfy everyone? What are the chances of success with such a solution? Overall, which alternative–destroying the Notice of Assignment or a "win-win" solution–has greater risk?

3. If Craig, who is Susan's superior, orders Susan to destroy the Notice of Assignment and deny that she had ever seen it, what should she do? She is not only an individual with her own sense of integrity and right conduct, but she is also an employee, who has an obligation to follow orders and work for the best interests of the company.

Case Objectives

This case illustrates several important points. First, it shows that unethical conduct may be perceived as a solution to managerial mistakes. The temptation to destroy the Notice of Assignment would not have arisen had Susan and Craig been aware of it and acted accordingly. Second, the case raises the problem of taking full responsibility in situations where others also bear some responsibility. If Susan and Craig attempt to find an ethical solution, they risk taking full responsibility for a problem to which both TekUSA and Mr. Hayes have contributed. Third, the case invites creative problem solving. There may be a "win-win" solution that will satisfy everyone. However, the unethical alternative is easy and reasonably safe, whereas any other solution is difficult and uncertain.

TEACHING STRATEGIES

1. The first class session is critical for setting the tone of the course. Rather than lecturing on "What Is Business Ethics," many experienced instructors prefer to explain by doing, that is by plunging into a discussion of substantive ethical problems. A good "starter" case is "Kate Simpson" in *Cases in Ethics and the Conduct of Business*. Video cases are especially effective for the first class session, and the instructor has many from which to choose. (See the section of this manual "A Note on Sources.") Arthur Andersen & Co. has produced a 25-minute videotape, "Ethics in Business," in which business executives talk about the importance of ethics in business and several young people describe ethical dilemmas that they have faced.

2. Introduce business ethics by writing "business" on one half of the board and "ethics" on the other. Define each by asking what words or phrases they bring to mind, and then ask what these words or phrases might have to do with one another. In this way, the instructor can explore the question of whether business ethics is an oxymoron. Students are likely to move from economic descriptions of business ("make a profit") to more personal descriptions (such as "leading people" and "finding fulfilling work"), at which point the instructor can ask what is involved in leading people or being fulfilled. Some descriptions of business are apt to convey metaphors, such as "Business is a game" or "It's a jungle out there," which can be examined. Some useful reading for preparing this lesson includes Albert Carr's classic article "Is Business Bluffing Ethical?" which is widely reprinted, and chapter 2 "Macho Myths and Metaphors" in Robert C. Solomon, *Ethics and Excellence* (New York: Oxford University Press, 1993). The views of Carr and Solomon, which can be easily summarized, provide clear contrasts.

3. If students have some business experience, then it may be useful to draw out their perceptions of ethics in business based on this experience. A resource is the article "Business Ethics: A View from the Trenches" by Joseph L. Badaracco, Jr., and James Webb, in *California Management Review*, 37 (1995), 8-28. The authors found that many young managers they interviewed had been ordered or felt strong pressure to commit unethical and sometimes illegal acts, that they believed that higher-ups were "out of touch" on ethical issues, that corporate guidelines, such as codes of ethics and corporate ethics programs, were of little use in resolving dilemmas, and that they relied instead on their own judgments and values. The interviewees also concluded that one should not "overinvest" in ethics. One strategy is to compare the responses of students in class with those in the study.

4. Although Part I of the text is devoted to ethical theory, these chapters need not be covered in their entirety before the remaining chapters are assigned. The material on ethical theory can be introduced gradually along with substantive business ethics problems, and some instructors may choose to include only a minimal amount of theory. The text is flexible enough to permit a variety of choices regarding the treatment of ethical theory.

5. The role of fairness in market exchanges is illustrated by the "ultimatum bargaining game." In this game, two people are given a certain amount of money (say $10) on the condition that one person proposes how the money is to be divided (for example, $5 to each) and the second person accepts or rejects the proposed division. The first person can make only one proposal, and if the proposal is rejected by the second person, the money is taken away and each person receives nothing. Economic theory suggests that the second person would accept any proposal, no matter how small the share, if the alternative is no money at all. Hence, the first person could offer to share as little as $1 or less. But many people who play the game will refuse a proposal in which they receive a share that is considered too small and hence unfair. The results of experiments with the ultimatum bargaining game are presented in Robert H. Frank, *Passions within Reason: The Strategic Role of the Emotions* (New York: Norton, 1988), 170-74. For a discussion of the implications for business ethics, see Norman E. Bowie, "Challenging the Egoistic Paradigm," *Business Ethics Quarterly*, 1 (1991), 1-21. Instructors with ample resources might play the game with students, while those less well endowed might choose merely to explain the game.

KEY TERMS AND CONCEPTS

business ethics

business system level

cultural relativism

descriptive ethics

economic point of view

economic efficiency

equity/efficiency trade-off

ethical displacement

ethical management

ethical theory

ethical relativism

ethics

externalities

fiduciary duty

free market

good faith

individual level

integrated approach

justification

legal point of view

management of ethics

market imperfections

moral principles

moral reasoning

moral point of view

moral judgment

morality

normative ethics

organizational level

CHAPTER TWO

UTILITARIANISM

CHAPTER SUMMARY

Utilitarianism is a powerful and widely accepted ethical theory that has special relevance to problems in business. It provides a fairly straightforward decision making process to assist in determining the best course of action in many situations. Its application involves developing a list of available alternatives, following the consequences of each as far into the future as possible, and selecting the alternative with the greatest balance of benefits over harms for everyone. Chapter 2 also introduces the distinction between teleological and deontological theories and explores the strengths and weakness of both kinds of theories for the purposes of business ethics.

CHAPTER OVERVIEW

Two Types of Ethical Theories

It is customary to divide ethical theories into *teleological* and *deontological*. The most prominent example of a teleological theory is utilitarianism, while the best-known deontological theory is Kant's. A third type of ethical theory, known as *virtue ethics*, is discussed in the next chapter.

Teleological theories. These hold that the rightness of an action is determined solely by its consequences. In classical utilitarianism, pleasure is the only ultimate good and pain the only evil. Other utilitarian theories, however, offer different accounts of what constitutes good and bad consequences. In general, all utilitarian theories define good on the basis of each person's conception of what it means to be better off. Teleological theories have two strengths. First, they fit with much of our ordinary moral reasoning and thus can explain why truth-telling, promise-keeping, respect for property, and so on, are right actions. On the other hand, teleological theories can also explain why lying can occasionally be the right thing to do. Second, teleological theories provide a relatively precise and objective method for moral decision-making in which one need only calculate the consequences of the available alternatives. Much of our moral reasoning is non-teleological in nature. For example, we generally are obliged to keep our promises, even when more good might be achieved by breaking them. In additional, role obligations, such as those assumed by parents toward their children, are difficult to justify on purely teleological grounds. And the concepts of rights and justice are a difficult challenge for teleological theories.

Deontological theories. Deontological theories ignore the consequences of actions and focus on the nature of the actions and the rules from which they follow. The Golden Rule and ethical principles that appeal to both human dignity and respect are both deontological in nature. W.D. Ross formulates seven rules or duties: fidelity, reparation, gratitude, justice, beneficence, self-improvement, and nonmaleficence. Two strengths of the deontological approach are that it makes sense of cases in which consequences seem to be irrelevant and it accounts for the role of motives

13

in evaluating actions. A weakness of the deontological approach is its failure to provide a plausible explanation for how we know our moral obligations and how we resolve cases of conflict among our obligations. Ross, for example, suggests no order of priority among the rules. Even though he distinguishes between actual and prima facie obligations, we may have several incompatible prima facie obligations in any given situation and no way to determine which is our actual duty.

Classical Utilitarianism

Different parts of the utilitarian doctrine were advanced by ancient Greek philosophers, but it wasn't until the early nineteenth century that two English reformers fashioned the various utilitarian pieces into a coherent whole. These two philosophers were Jeremy Bentham (1748-1832) and John Stuart Mill (1806-1873). Bentham's utilitarianism approves of actions that augment, and disapproves of actions that diminish, the happiness of the party in question. He measured this amount of pleasure or pain by a hedonistic calculus that considers such factors as intensity, duration, likelihood of occurrence, and proximity in time. According to Bentham, if this process is repeated for all individuals, the resulting sums will show the good or bad tendency of an action for an entire community. However, critics charge that his conception of pleasure is too crude to constitute the sole good for human beings. Mill modified Bentham's utilitarianism by proposing that actions are right inasmuch as they promote happiness and wrong inasmuch as they promote the opposite of happiness. Happiness is pleasure and the absence of pain. In addition, he stipulated that pleasures differ in their quality, so that humans enjoy higher pleasures than animals. One can argue that Mill saves hedonism from the charge of crudeness because the higher pleasures enjoyed by a few with elevated tastes are unlikely to outweigh the total sum of the base pleasures enjoyed by most. Mill gives us no guidance for comparing the quality with the quantity of pleasure. However, in other writings Mill seems to claim that the development of our critical faculties and the capacity for autonomous action are ends in themselves.

The Forms of Utilitarianism

According to classical utilitarianism an action is right if, and only if, it produces the greatest balance of pleasure over pain for everyone. This formula makes utilitarianism *consequentialist* (it relies on consequences), *hedonist* (it identifies the good with pleasure and the absence of pain), *maximalist* (it must have not just *some* good consequences, but the *greatest* amount of good consequences), and *universalist* (the consequences for everyone must be considered). Universalism also demands that we be impartial, regarding each person's interest equally, including our own. The utilitarian principle does not insist that the interests of everyone be promoted; they oblige us only to include the interests of everyone in our calculations.

Act- and rule-utilitarianism. Act-utilitarianism evaluates the rightness of any given act by the consequences of that act. Rule utilitarianism determines the rightness of an act by appealing to a relevant rule of morality, which in turn is justified by the consequences of observing that rule. Act- and rule-utilitarianism each has its merits, and there is no consensus among philosophers about which is correct.

Problems with calculating utility. Classical utilitarianism requires that we be able to determine both the amount of utility for each individual affected by an action, and the amount of utility for a whole society. Thus, a vast amount of information is needed. Moreover, interpersonal comparisons of utility raises theoretical problems that challenge whether the calculations required by utilitarianism are even possible, although we make these comparisons in practice.

Cost-Benefit Analysis

Bentham's idea of a precise quantitative method for decision making is most fully realized in a cost-benefit analysis. In cost-benefit analysis, monetary units are used to express the benefits and drawbacks of various alternatives in a decision making process. The chief advantage of cost-benefit analysis is that the prices of many goods are set by the market, which eliminates the need to have knowledge of people's pleasures or preference rankings. Because of its narrow focus on economic efficiency in the allocation of resources, cost-benefit analysis is not commonly used as a basis for personal morality. In addition, it cannot determine such moral questions as the rights of consumers in matters of product safety or environmental protection but can be used only to determine appropriate levels of both product safety and environmental protection. A distinction can be made between *cost-benefit analysis*, which is used to select both the means to an end and the end itself, and *cost-effectiveness analysis*, which assumes that we already have some agreed-upon end, and the only question regards the most efficient means of achieving it.

The problems of assigning monetary values. Not all costs and benefits have an easily determined monetary value; examples include the enjoyment of family and friends, peace and quiet, police protection, and freedom from the risk of injury and death. Moreover, the market price of a good does not always correspond to its *opportunity cost*. For example, the fact that a yacht costs more than a college education does not mean that consumers value yachts more highly than education. One can attempt to overcome these problems through *shadow pricing*. This approach enables a value to be placed on goods that reflects people's market and non-market behavior. For example, by comparing the prices of houses near airports with the prices of similar houses elsewhere, it is possible to infer the value that people place on peace and quiet. But there are limitations. Someone who buys a house near an airport may be unable to afford comparable housing elsewhere or simply may not mind the noise.

Should all things be assigned a monetary value? Some argue that placing a dollar value on certain goods actually lessens their perceived value, since they are valued precisely because they *cannot* be bought or sold. Friendship, love, and life itself are examples of such goods. Such arguments are beside the point, because cost-benefit analysis requires that a value be placed on goods only for the purposes of calculation.

Other values in cost-benefit analysis. Though cost-benefit analysis purports to be value-free, critics claim that it is heavily value-laden because analysts cannot entirely disengage their own values from the analysis. Before such an investigation begins, the analyst must make several value-laden decisions, including:

1. The range of alternatives to be considered in the analysis.
2. What constitutes a cost and a benefit as well as whose values determine this.
3. What counts as a consequence of a particular act.
4. The number of "spillover effects" or externalities that are included.

5. The distance into the future that the consequences are calculated.

In the end we must remember that cost-benefit analysis is only as good as the analyst who performs it and that this method is not intended to be the sole means for arriving at important decisions we make as a society.

CASE SUMMARIES

Case 2.1 Lockheed in Japan

Lockheed was in dire financial straits and needed to sell a number of its new L-1011 passenger jets to All Nippon Airways. Lockheed's president, Carl Kotchian, was told that in order to set up a crucial meeting with the prime minister of Japan, he had to promise to pay a substantial amount of money, which he agreed to do. In the end, Lockheed paid about $12.5 million in bribes and commissions to sell 21 L-1011 jets in Japan. Lockheed also paid bribes totaling more than $30 million to Italian and Netherlands officials regarding other plane contracts. None of these payments violated American law at the time. Kotchian justified his decision by citing the benefits to Lockheed employees and shareholders among others, the fact that the payments were demanded by the Japanese and not offered by Lockheed, and the need to make such payments in order to make sales in a country where bribery was practiced.

Discussion Questions

1. Was Kotchian simply doing what any good business executive would do and indeed what is required of his role? Would he be failing to do his job as president of Lockheed if he refused to pay on the grounds that bribery is wrong?
2. Who was really harmed by Lockheed's bribes? Since the bribes amounted to a scant three percent of the expected sum of sales from the 21 planes, could the bribes be justified as a reasonable cost of doing business?
3. Does it make any difference that Kotchian himself never offered the bribes and that the bribes were demanded by the Japanese? Were the payments bribes or money that was extorted from the company? Is there anything wrong with making payments in response to cases of extortion?
4. Do the facts that bribery is an accepted practice in many parts of the world and a necessity for selling airplanes in Japan make it more justifiable? Ask students whether they accept Kotchian's defense that the company did not approve of bribery but had no choice.
5. Should there be a law that prohibits bribery by U.S. companies?

Case Objectives

This case illustrates the correct and incorrect use of utilitarianism to make a business decision and, in particular, the different results of applying the two versions of the utilitarian principle. Act-utilitarianism might seem to justify the payment of the bribes because of the obvious benefit to Lockheed employees, suppliers, stockholders, and the United States as a whole. The harms are less obvious but still substantial: Lockheed's actions harmed their competitors who lost sales, the incident caused a scandal in Japan with far-reaching consequences, and arguably U.S. commercial and foreign policy interests were damaged. Thus, there is a need to examine all of the consequences of an act. The wrongfulness of Lockheed's action may not be fully revealed, however, until the analysis is shifted to the consequences of bribery as a practice, which is to apply rule-utilitarianism to the case.

The case can be used to explore the nature of role morality. Ask students to imagine what Kotchian could say to Lockheed employees and shareholders if he had refused to pay the bribes. In addition, the use of the legal point of view can be explored in this case. Although Lockheed's action was legal at the time, it prompted the Foreign Corrupt Practices Act, which now prohibits bribery by American companies. A discussion of the justification of this law leads to many issues covered in Chapter 15 on international business.

Case 2.2 Declining Sales at Supravac

Supravac had an unusual problem. The company's vacuum cleaners were so well made that they lasted a long time, and as a result sales of its new machines were lagging. In response Supravac proposed to build machines that would last only eight years—which is a practice known as planned obsolescence—in order to sell more and keep its workforce employed.

Discussion Questions

1. If planned obsolescence produces benefits for the employees that outweigh the losses to consumers, would not a utilitarian favor Evans's proposal?
2. Has Evans considered all of the costs? What might he be overlooking?
3. If the company is prepared to spend $3 million dollars, is there any alternative to cheapening the product that might produce the same or a greater return? If so, which plan would a utilitarian adopt?
4. Even if planned obsolescence would benefit shareholders eleven years later, would this plan be fair to current shareholders? What if the payoff were twenty years later, or fifty years later?

Case Objectives

The employees and stockholders of Supravac benefit from the planned obsolescence, while the consumers do not. At first glance, the case seems to involve a difficult trade-off that poses a utilitarianism problem, especially insofar as the theory justifies a possibly unethical practice. But the fact that three million dollars could be spent on some other alternative shows that utilitarianism is being misapplied because a utilitarian must consider all of the available alternatives. Still, if planned obsolescence is "ripping off the customer," then it might appear to be objectionable for nonutilitarian reasons. This issue can be examined by pointing out that no product is made as well as it could be and that all manufacturers have to decide how well a product should be made. Ask students how this decision should be made.

Case 2.3 Exporting Pollution

In a memo, Jim Donnelly argues that the case for locating a new chemical plant in a poor, third world country is supported by cost-benefit analysis because: (1) pollution does less harm in a less polluted country than in a more polluted one; (2) any harm done to poor people results in less cost;

(3) fewer cancers will occur in a poor country in which people die young from other causes; and the cost of pollution is a function of the amount that people are willing to pay for such things as clean air, and rich people will pay more. Rebecca Wright, who is a specialist in cost-benefit analysis, is troubled by the conclusion but can find little fault in the reasoning.

Discussion Questions

1. Why does the memo trouble Rebecca Wright?
2. Would the memo be less troubling if the question were whether to place a toxic waste dump in a large urban area or a largely unpopulated area of the United States? Does the fact that the proposal involves the export of pollution from the first world to the third world make a difference?
3. Is the memo troubling because the people of the third world do not have an opportunity to take part in the decision? Would the case be different if the people affected recognized the benefits and consented to the location of the plant in their country?

Case Objectives

This case is based on an actual memo by an official at the World Bank that caused a great stir when it was leaked to the press. As an example of cost-benefit analysis, the reasoning is sound, so challenge students to find any fault. The main problem lies with the *distribution* of costs and benefits. If cost-benefit analysis is used for a broad range of public policy questions, then people in any given country are benefited and harmed in almost equal measure. The distribution of benefits and harms between the rich and poor countries, however, is apt to be skewed consistently in favor of the rich. Is this fair? In addition, the people of third world countries often have no opportunity to give their consent. Americans do not explicitly consent to all decisions made by cost-benefit analysis, but students might be asked whether we have consented at least to the use of this method for decision making. Would it be rational for people in third world countries to consent to the use of cost-benefit analysis?

TEACHING STRATEGIES

1. The purpose of this chapter is not to investigate the intricacies of utilitarianism, as one would in a course on ethical theory, but rather to understand the theory as a practical decision making tool and a basis for public policy. Students who lack a background in ethics may have difficulty understanding some of the concepts. Instructors will have to decide how much emphasis to place on theoretical understanding and how much to place on the ability of students to use utilitarian reasoning in practice. This is a good time in the course to assign a short paper in which students are asked to describe utilitarianism and apply utilitarian reasoning to a specific case.

2. Utilitarianism is a very *demanding* ethical theory. Many students mistakenly believe that utilitarianism can be reduced to the claim that any action that maximizes profit for a business is ethical. It is easy to forget that utilitarianism demands that ethical agents be *impartial* and seek the well-being of everyone. Students can be asked whether utilitarianism is too demanding for ordinary human beings and whether the theory would require corporations to be concerned with overall social welfare. Instructors who are familiar with the debate over particularism and universalism, may want to explore how parents can be justified in favoring the welfare of their own children over other children—or corporations in favoring shareholders over other constituencies.

3. Because of its relevance to business decision making, some instructors may want to focus primarily on cost-benefit analysis. An example of an actual analysis is helpful for leading a discussion. Especially recommended is the analysis that Ford Motor Company conducted for the Ford Pinto in 1973, which is reproduced on the next page. (This analysis is often misrepresented in discussions of the Ford Pinto case, and so instructors may want to research the relevant background.) Students often take the position that *no* monetary value can be assigned to life, but ask students how decisions about the large number of possible safety improvements ought to be made. The discussion can be furthered by pointing out that lower speed limits save lives and asking, What would be the "ideal" speed limit? Boatright defends the placing of a monetary value on life in cost-benefit analysis and cites estimates that the value of life for most Americans is about $10 million. Ask students to evaluate Boatright's arguments and the basis for the $10 million figure.

KEY TERMS AND CONCEPTS

act-utilitarianism
consequentialism
cost-benefit analysis
cost-effectiveness analyses
deontological theories
externalities
hedonism
hedonistic calculus
interpersonal comparison of utility
maximalism
opportunity costs
ordinal and cardinal values
rule-utilitarianism
shadow pricing
teleological theories
universalism
utilitarianism
utility

COST-BENEFIT ANALYSIS

The following is from a study of the costs and benefits of installing an $11 valve on all Ford cars to prevent the leakage of fuel in the event of a rollover. The cost-benefit analysis was released by the Ford Motor Company in an effort to show that a more stringent government standard for fuel leakage in rollover accidents was unwarranted. Source: "Fatalities Associated with Crash Induced Fuel Leakages and Fires," Ford Motor Company, September 19, 1973.

BENEFITS

Savings:	180 burn deaths, 180 serious injuries, 2,100 burned vehicles
Unit Cost:	$200,000 per death, $67,000 per injury, $700 per vehicle
Total Benefit:	$180 \times \$200,000 + 180 \times \$67,000 + 2,100 \times \$700 = \$49.5$ million

COSTS

Sales:	11 million cars, 1.5 million light trucks
Unit Cost:	$11 per car, $11 per truck
Total Cost:	$11,000,000 \times \$11 + 1,500,000 \times \$11 = \$137$ million

The figure of $200,000 as the cost of each death was taken from a NHTSA study which broke down the estimated costs as follows:

COMPONENT	1971 COST
Future productivity losses	
Direct	$132,000
Indirect	41,300
Medical costs	
Hospital	700
Other	425
Property damage	1,500
Insurance administration	4,700
Legal and court	3,000
Employer losses	1,000
Victim's pain and suffering	10,000
Funeral	900
Assets (lost consumption)	5,000
Miscellaneous	200
TOTAL PER FATALITY	$200,725

CHAPTER THREE

KANTIAN ETHICS, RIGHTS, AND VIRTUE

CHAPTER SUMMARY

This chapter examines two nonutilitarian approaches to ethics that do not appeal to consequences, namely *Kantian ethics* and *virtue ethics*. Kantian ethics is perhaps the best developed and most widely accepted version of a deontological theory, although virtue ethics has received renewed attention. Chapter 3 concludes with a discussion of the meaning of *rights* and the different foundations that have been offered for them.

CHAPTER OVERVIEW

Introduction

Kant's moral philosophy, which is presented mainly in the *Groundwork of the Metaphysics of Morals* (1785), is based not on consequences but on human reason, which Kant believed has the power to discover a moral law that is binding on all rational persons. Consider someone who wants to make a false promise in order to borrow some much needed money. Kant held that even if the person could do more good by borrowing the money under false pretenses, the action would still be wrong. Moreover, he denied that any consequence, such as pleasure, could be good in itself. The only thing that can be good without qualification is *good will*, which is a matter of performing an action solely because it is a person's duty.

The Categorical Imperative

The fundamental principle of morality in Kantian ethics is the *categorical imperative*, which is: Act only according to that maxim by which you can at the same time will that it should become a universal law. Kant explained the categorical principle by means of the moral and nonmoral uses of the word *ought*. Used in the *nonmoral* sense, *ought* issues in what Kant called hypothetical imperatives that take the form "if you want x, then do y." Kant believed that *ought* used in the moral sense involves categorical imperatives of the form "Do y," without any reference to empirical conditions, such as desires. How do we identify these imperatives? According to Kant, these are rules (or maxims) that a rational person could will everyone to follow, and acts that follow these rules are right. Immoral acts, by contrast, follow rules that, if followed by everyone, would be self-defeating in some way. Kant has been called a "closet utilitarian," however, he does not appeal to the undesirable consequences of a bad maxim but rather to the sheer impossibility of its being followed by everyone.

Many ethicists who reject categorical imperatives still agree that all moral judgments must be *universalizable*. Universalizability can be expressed in two ways. First, we have to say that an action that is right for one person must be right for all other similar persons in similar circumstances.

This counters a natural temptation to make exceptions for ourselves or to apply double standards. Second, the principle is the basis of the common question, "What if everyone did that?" This question refers to hypothetical rather than actual consequences and suggests that if not everyone could perform some act, then that act is wrong. Universalizability is incapable of refuting fanatics, such as a Nazi who wishes everyone to persecute Jews even if it should be proved that he is a Jew himself.

Respect for Persons

The second formulation of the categorical imperative is: Act so that you treat humanity, whether in your own person or in that of another, always as an end and never as a means only. This principle is often expressed as a duty to respect persons. Virtually all ethical systems involve a respect for persons, but the Kantian argument for this duty is distinctive. Reason, in Kant's view, enables human beings to act freely, to have *autonomy*, and so to respect other people is to respect their capacity for reason or their autonomy. The principle of respect for persons does not lend itself to a precise method for decision making. For example, respect for employees would entail a high degree of job security, but the principle does not tell us how to manage the inevitable trade-offs with such factors as decreased efficiency. The principle of respect for persons might seem to be superior to utilitarianism in cases where utilitarians are willing to sacrifice the interests of a few in order to increase the welfare of many, but in other cases increased welfare might take precedence over respect for persons. For example, utilitarianism would generally support paternalistic legislation to protect worker health and safety, whereas the principle of respect for persons would generally allow workers to decide whether they want to be protected. Arguably, workers ought to be protected by law rather than given a choice.

The Concept of a Right

The concept of rights emerges in many discussions of ethics and public policy. Both employers and employees are commonly regarded as having certain rights. However, these various rights must be carefully distinguished for several reasons.

1. The concept is used in many different ways, yielding different interpretations.
2. Rights can come into conflict with one another.
3. Because of the moral significance we attach to rights, there is a tendency to stretch the concept of a right in ways that dilute its meaning.
4. Rational persons can disagree about the existence of a particular right, such as the right of all persons to receive adequate food, clothing, and medical care.

Rights can be understood as *entitlements* that enable us to act on our own and be treated by others in a certain way, without asking permission or being dependent on other people's good will.

Some distinctions between rights

1. *Legal rights and moral rights.* Legal rights are rights that are recognized and enforced as part of a legal system. Moral rights do not depend on a legal system but are the rights people morally ought to have.

2. *In rem and in personam rights.* Rights that involve claims on specific identifiable individuals are called *in personam* rights. Other rights are general or *in rem* rights since they involve claims against humanity in general.

3. *Negative and positive rights.* Negative rights entail an obligation on the part of others to refrain from acting in certain ways. Positive rights, such as a right to education, impose obligations on others to provide us with some good or service and thereby act positively on our behalf.

The Foundation of Rights

Discovering a foundation for rights raises the following question. Are rights fundamental moral categories with their own foundation or are they founded on a more general ethical theory, such as utilitarianism or Kantian ethics?

Natural rights theory. Natural rights, which are also called human rights, belong to all persons solely by virtue of being human. They are characterized by two features. They are *universal*, because they are possessed by all persons; and they are *unconditional* (or inalienable), because they do not depend on any particular practices or social institutions. The idea of natural rights goes back to the ancient Greeks who held that there is a higher law that applies to all persons at all times and places. Locke supported the idea of natural rights by describing a *state of nature*, which is the condition of human beings in the absence of any government. He held that humans have rights even in the state of nature and that the main reason for forming a government is to preserve these rights. The most important natural right, for Locke, is the right to *property*. Locke's theory of natural rights represents a significant advance over the traditional natural law theory, and the particular rights listed by Locke are precisely those required for the operation of a free market. Unfortunately, Locke's version of natural rights theory does not provide an adequate foundation for the wide range of rights that exist in modern society.

Utility and rights. It is often charged that utilitarianism cannot provide a foundation for rights; but Bentham and Mill both provide a theory of rights, and several contemporary utilitarian justifications have been developed. Mill urged that we develop practices and institutions to guide us in socially beneficial ways. Rights facilitate such an *indirect pursuit of utility*, especially in situations where substantial considerations of human welfare are at stake and the benefit of respecting rights is difficult to see. A good example of a utilitarian defense of rights is Mill's argument that denying the right of free speech runs the risk of suppressing not only falsehoods but also the truth.

A Kantian foundation for rights. Kant himself did not devote much attention to rights, though many of his followers have. Kant distinguished between *innate* rights, which belong to everyone, and *acquired* rights, which depend on some human convention or judicial act. In Kant's view, innate rights are derived from the human capacity to be rational agents and act autonomously. Innate rights are by definition those that are in accord with universal law, as expressed by the categorical imperative. Kant realized that in order for humans to be rational agents, they had to be free from certain limitations imposed by the will of others. Therefore, there is one fundamental innate right: the right to be free from the constraint of the will of others. From this fundamental right, Kant derived additional subsidiary rights, including the right to equal treatment, equal opportunity, and the ownership of property. The fundamental right that freedom from the constraint of the will of others supports is excessively narrow. Kant argues primarily for negative rights of non-interference rather than the positive rights of welfare. Kant's foundation for rights provides few resources for determining just what rights humans actually have. If rights are minimal conditions, then they run the risk of justifying too little, but if rights are maximal conditions, then they are in danger of justifying too much.

Virtue Ethics

The idea of virtue in business is not hopelessly out of place, because virtuous characteristics can lead not only to personal success in a career but to the successful operation of a business. Central to virtue ethics is the idea that morality is not performing certain right actions but possessing a certain character. Instead of asking, "What actions are right?" virtue ethics asks, "What kind of persons should we be?" In the *Nicomachean Ethics*, Aristotle argued that ethics enables us to live the good life and that the good life is possible only for virtuous persons. Aristotle described particular virtues in illuminating detail. After Aristotle, philosophical theory tended to focus more on right action and duties, but some contemporary philosophers argue for a return to virtue ethics.

What are virtues? Virtues are specifically those traits that *everyone* needs for the good life, regardless of their specific situation. For example, courage is a virtue because it enables anyone to get what he or she wants. The virtues are integrally related to what Aristotle called practical wisdom, which is what a person needs in order to live well. Virtue is variously described as an *excellence* that is admired in a person, as a disposition to act in a certain way, and as a specific state of character. Lists of the virtues generally include: benevolence, compassion, courage, courtesy, dependability, friendliness, honesty, loyalty, moderation, self-control, and tolerance. In developing a list of virtues, we must consider not only the contribution of a virtue to some end but also the end itself. Aristotle considered happiness to be the end of life, and so the virtues must all contribute in some way to happiness. Thus, the character traits that enable a despot or a criminal or a lecher to be successful are not virtues because they do not conduce to happiness. Moreover, the virtues are not merely means to happiness but are themselves constitutive of it. For example, a parent cannot experience the joy of parenting without actually possessing the traits that make one a good parent.

Virtue ethics in business. Virtue ethics presupposes some end (happiness is the end of life for Aristotle), and so applying virtue ethics to business requires us to determine the *end* toward which business aims. Adopting an Aristotelian approach, Robert Solomon argues that the main purpose of business is not merely to create wealth but to enable us to live the good life. Thus, business is a matter of getting along with others, having a sense of self-respect, and taking pride in what we do. Business, from an Aristotelian point of view, is essentially a communal activity in which people work together for a common good. The virtues in business are those character traits that enable us to achieve this end of business. For the most part, these are the character traits necessary for everyday life, but some exceptions must be made. For example, honesty in business is compatible with a certain amount of concealment that is unacceptable in personal relations, and so the virtue of honesty must be redefined for the purposes of business.

Strengths and weaknesses of virtue ethics. A strength of virtue ethics is that it fits with our everyday moral experience. The response of most people to a complex ethical dilemma is not to think about how universal principles can be applied but to decide what they feel comfortable with or what a person they admire would do. Codes of professional ethics generally stress that a professional should be a person of integrity. Unlike the impartiality stressed by utilitarianism and Kantianism, virtue ethics makes better sense of the role that *personal relations* play in morality. Since business activity is based so heavily on roles and relationships, in which such concepts as loyalty and trust figure prominently, virtue ethics is highly relevant to the workplace. A weakness of virtue ethics is its *incompleteness*. Virtue ethics can take us only so far in dealing with genuine ethical dilemmas. Some dilemmas involve the limits of rules (such as when concealing information becomes a lie) or conflicts between rules (when telling the truth would harm an innocent person, for example). Moreover, there are some difficult ethical dilemmas to which virtues do not readily apply. Some virtue ethicists respond that the importance of dilemmas in ethics has been overstated and that ethics is concerned primarily with the problems of everyday life. Another weakness is that virtue ethics does not address the problem of *conflict*. According to Aristotle, happiness is possible for anyone who becomes a certain kind of person, but insofar as our goals in life include possessing limited goods, not everyone can be successful. Virtue ethicists respond that morality is more a matter of living cooperatively than of moderating conflict.

CASE SUMMARIES

Case 3.1 Big Brother at Procter & Gamble

The CEO of Procter and Gamble (P&G), Edward Artz, was angered by leaks to the *Wall Street Journal* about the forced resignation of an executive vice president over problems in the food and beverage division. In an attempt to find the source of the leaks, Artz persuaded the local county prosecutor to open a grand jury investigation and to conduct a search of telephone company records to uncover any calls to *Journal* reporter Alecia Swasy. Ohio law prohibits employees from disclosing "confidential information" without the permission of their employer, but reporters are generally protected by the First Amendment right of freedom of the press. Moreover, information about an executive's forced departure is scarcely a trade secret protectable by law. Many objected to P&G's action as an abuse of power and a violation of the rights of privacy and speech.

Discussion Questions

1. Was P&G justified in investigating its own employees in order to find the source of a suspected leak? Do you agree with Artz that a company has a right to protect its secrets? Does this right depend on the kind of information that a company seeks to protect?
2. If P&G had a right to investigate, is there a limit to the steps that it can take? Suppose P&G had searched only the company's own telephone records, or confined its search to the home telephone records of P&G employees. Would the company have kept within permissible limits?
3. Were the rights of Cincinnati area residents violated by the check of their telephone records? How would you feel if your own telephone records were checked in this way?
4. Do you agree with Artz's claim that his actions involved mistakes of judgment but were not "an issue of ethics?"

The Procter & Gamble case illustrates the importance of rights in business ethics. The company justified the investigation by appealing to a right to protect its secrets, while critics charged that people's rights of privacy and free speech were violated. Thus, the case provides an opportunity both to examine theoretical questions about rights and to evaluate arguments that appeal to rights. In particular, rights have boundaries, and many disputes concern the drawing of these boundaries. P&G may have a right to investigate the source of leaks, but how far is the company justified in going? The case raises issues of corporate relations with the media and with local government that some instructors may want to explore. Although lying to a reporter is generally wrong, did Artz have any obligation to confirm the story or to reveal additional information? If Artz sought to punish the *Wall Street Journal* by leaking news to rival newspapers, was he being unethical or merely playing hardball?

Case 3.2 Clean Hands in a Dirty Business

Janet Moore's only job prospect is in the marketing department of Union Tobacco Company, which produces snuff in forms that are designed to hook young boys. Her friend Karen, who works at Union Tobacco, shares Janet's repulsion at the company's pitch to youngsters but points out that she has scuttled many objectionable advertising ploys. Karen argues that if Janet does not take the job, it will be filled by someone with fewer scruples. By taking the job, Janet may prevent some harm that would otherwise occur, but she will also be contributing directly to diseases among young boys and even some deaths.

Discussion Questions

1. Is Karen's argument persuasive? Should Janet consider, as morally relevant, the lessening of harm that she can achieve?

2. Should the fact that she will now bear some responsibility for the harm done also be a consideration in her thinking? Would Janet bear some responsibility for the harm done if she declined the job and thereby the opportunity to make a difference?

3. If you were in Janet's position, would you be concerned about the "fit" between this job and your own character, and how the job might *change* your character? Would it be important if you could not take pride in your work and derive satisfaction from it?

4. Machiavelli asserted that an effective leader must "know how to do wrong," not for his own good but for the good of the state. Do you agree with this claim about politics? Does the claim also hold true for business, or are there some significant differences between politics and business?

Case Objectives

This case illustrates the classic "dirty hands" problem, which is much discussed in government ethics. Is it better to allow greater harm to be done by others, where one is not responsible, or to act yourself to reduce the harm but be responsible for the harm done? The "dirty hands" problem reveals a division between utilitarianism on the one hand and Kantian ethics and virtue ethics on the other. Insofar as utilitarianism considers only consequences, the theory would seem to justify taking the job; but by doing so, Janet would be assuming responsibility for the harm done. Kantian ethics and virtue ethics, for different reasons, would make personal responsibility and not consequences the primary consideration. An important difference between this case and Machiavelli's point that a leader must "know how to do wrong" is that having dirty hands may be necessary for a political leader and perhaps, a business leader, but not for an ordinary citizen or employee.

Case 3.3 An Auditor's Dilemma

Alison Lloyd's job is to verify all expenditures for Gem Packing. Noticing a sizable invoice from Ace Glass Company on June 10 for July and August deliveries that have not yet been made, she approached Greg Berg, the head of purchasing, who explained the situation to her. Gem's jam and jelly division operates under an incentive plan whereby managers receive substantial bonuses for meeting their profit quota for the fiscal year ending June 30. Missing quota is considered a death blow to the career of an aspiring, young executive, while nothing is gained from exceeding a quota. So after meeting a quota, some managers would attempt to prepay as many expenses as possible in order to work toward next year's goal. The shipping department also helps out by delaying orders or by postdating the delivery dates. The company's top management is apparently unaware of these practices, but they designed the incentive plan and have been satisfied with the results.

Discussion Questions

1. Is any harm really being done by the practices at Gem? Who, if anyone, is harmed, and how serious is the harm? Could the situation "spin out of control?" If so, what could be the potential consequences?

2. What, if anything, might happen if the practices became publicly known? If you were a member of top management, how would you view the situation, and how would you deal with it?

3. Alison is a member of the Institute of Internal Auditors, which has a code of ethics that requires members to exercise "honesty, objectivity, and diligence" in their duties, while remaining loyal to their employers. What should she do after she becomes aware of the situation? As a professional, does she have a responsibility to the public as well as to her employer?

4. Who is responsible for this situation—the lower-level managers who circumvent the incentive plan or the top managers who designed it and implemented the plan?

Case Objectives

This case concerns (1) the importance of financial controls in a corporation, (2) the ethical dimension of corporate policies, especially those that produce unintended unethical behavior, and (3) the place of professional ethics in a corporate setting. The scenario closely resembles a crisis at H.J. Heinz Company that is described in a widely used Harvard Business School case, "H.J. Heinz Company (A)." Instructors may want to examine that case in full and consult the teaching note that accompanies it. Although the practices at Gem may appear to be harmless, the consequences of lax financial controls are potentially very serious. The case provides an opportunity to explore the value of reliable financial information for both the company and the financial markets. The incentive plan was not well-designed and implemented, and so the responsibility of top management for unethical conduct in the organization can be examined. Finally, the fact that Alison Lloyd is a professional and a member of a professional organization with a code of ethics introduces the important element of professional ethics.

TEACHING STRATEGIES

1. After students have been introduced to the various theories of ethics, have them discuss or write a paper on the similarities and differences in the application of the theories to a sample business ethics problem. A useful question is, do the theories lead to fundamentally different ways of reasoning, or do they lead in practice to similar ways of reasoning?

2. Responsibility raises many difficult problems that are not addressed in the text. Instructors who want to explore these problems further can use, in addition to Case 3.2 "Clean Hands in a Dirty Business," the "Kate Simpson" case in *Cases in Ethics and the Conduct of Business*. Ask students whether Kate herself is participating in the wrongdoing since she is merely delivering an envelope as requested. More complex questions about responsibility in large organizations are raised in the "Parable of the Sadhu," *Harvard Business Review* (September-October 1983), 103-188. A videotape on the "Parable of the Sadhu" is also available from Harvard Business School. The author, Bowen McCoy, describes how mountain climbers from different countries avoid responsibility for an unconscious Indian holy man who wandered into a remote Himalayan pass. The story, he believes, has many parallels for people in business.

3. At some point early in the course, the relevance of ethics to career development can be fruitfully introduced. Case 3.2 "Clean Hands in a Dirty Business" is clearly relevant. A longer, more complex case involving career development is "Dave Stewart" in the *Cases in Ethics and the Conduct of Business*. In "Dave Stewart (B)," available from Darden Educational Material Services, Dave leaves the Holmes Company for a new job, but his career is still jeopardized by his past service at Holmes.

4. Students are often divided on the importance of character in business and of having a job that fits with their own character. These questions can be explored by asking students whether they would consider the compromises that they might have to make in choosing a job, or whether companies should use character qualifications in hiring and promotion.

5. The text refers to feminist ethical theories in the context of virtue ethics but does not explain this approach to ethics. Using the works cited in the footnotes to the text, instructors may introduce this important movement and evaluate its applicability to business.

KEY TERMS AND CONCEPTS

Aristotle
autonomy
categorical and hypothetical imperatives
entitlements
good will
Immanuel Kant
in personam and *in rem* rights
innate and acquired rights
John Locke

legal and moral rights
natural (human) rights
paternalism
state of nature
the categorical imperative
universalizability
virtue

CHAPTER FOUR

JUSTICE AND THE MARKET SYSTEM

CHAPTER SUMMARY

Chapter 4 introduces the four principles of justice presented by Aristotle, Mill, Rawls, and Nozick, with a focus on distributive justice in a free market economy. Aristotle's principle of proportionate equality, the utilitarian justification of a principle of justice, Rawls's difference principle and his principle of equal opportunity, and Nozick's entitlement theory are all explained in order to provide a means for resolving issues involving justice. Finally, Adam Smith's defense of free markets and the libertarian justification of the market system are examined.

CHAPTER OVERVIEW

Justice is an important moral concept which can be used to evaluate individual actions as well as social, legal, political, and economic institutions. Justice applies to situations of distribution, such as the fair distribution of benefits and burdens. Justice also applies to the righting of wrongs, such as fair compensation for victims of wrongful harms and fair punishment for crimes. The concept of justice is relevant to business ethics primarily in terms of the distribution of benefits and burdens, although the justice of the economic system in which business activity takes place is also an important consideration in business ethics. In particular, the justification of a free market system includes criticisms and defenses of the system on the grounds of economic justice. Following are the four prominent theories of justice examined in the text:

1. Aristotle's principle of proportionate equality.
2. John Mill's theory of justice based on utility.
3. John Rawls's egalitarian theory of justice.
4. Robert Nozick's libertarian entitlement theory.

Aristotle's Analysis of Justice

In Book V of the *Nicomachean Ethics*, Aristotle distinguished *universal justice* and *particular justice*. Universal justice is the whole of virtue, while particular justice consists of taking only the proper share of some good or bearing a fair share of some burden. Aristotle divided particular justice into three distinct areas: distributive justice, compensatory justice, and retributive justice. *Distributive justice* deals with the distribution of benefits and burdens, mostly in the evaluation of social, political and economic institutions. *Compensatory justice* concerns the compensation of persons for wrongs done to them in voluntary relations such as contract breaches. And *retributive justice* involves the punishment of wrongdoers who have participated in involuntary relations such as criminal acts.

A just distribution can be one in which each person shares equally, but unequal sharing can also be considered just if the inequality is in accord with some principle of distribution. The *moral equilibrium,* or initial fair share of benefits and burdens, is upset when one person is made worse off by an accident where someone else is at fault or by a crime. Compensation and punishment restore the moral equilibrium by returning the victim to his or her previous condition or by punishing the perpetrator for the crime. Distributive justice is *comparative*. It considers not the absolute amount of benefits and burdens for each person, but each person's amount relative to that of others. Compensatory and retributive justice are both *noncomparative*. The amount of compensation or punishment is determined by the features of each case and not by a comparison with other cases.

The distinction has been made between *just procedures* and *just outcomes*, which is, to say, between the procedures used to distribute goods and the actual outcomes of those procedures. John Rawls further defines procedural justice as perfect, imperfect, and pure. *Perfect procedural justice* always produces a just outcome; *imperfect procedural justice* produces a just outcome only to a certain extent; and *pure procedural justice* is whatever results from following a given procedure because there is no independent criterion for a just outcome.

Aristotle on distributive justice. Aristotle's principle of justice is a moderate egalitarian position in which like cases should be treated alike unless there is some morally relevant difference between the cases. Aristotle adds that the difference in each person's share of a good must be proportional to his or her share of the relevant difference. This *principle of proportionate equality* is expressed by Aristotle in an arithmetic ratio in which two peoples' share of some good ought to be in proportion to their share of some relevant difference. Examples of such relevant differences are *ability, effort, accomplishment, contribution,* and *need.* The value of Aristotle's principle lies in its insistence that different treatments be justified by some relevant differences and that differences in treatment be in proportion to the relevant differences. The principle does not define these relevant differences nor does it resolve differences when they conflict.

Utility and Justice

Justice and rights pose a difficulty for utilitarianism, which would appear to favor any redistribution that increases total utility regardless of how it is accomplished. Thus, it is charged, utilitarianism places no value on equality and makes no allowance for justified unequal treatment. Bentham responds to the apparent conflict between utility and justice by asserting that equal distributions generally produce more utility than unequal ones, and so our ordinary views of justice rarely conflict with the utilitarian principle. When they do, however, equality ought to be sacrificed. Two arguments can be offered in support of this view regarding the convergence of utility and justice.

1. A system that maximizes utility tends toward equality in distribution (and thus toward the convergence of utility and justice) because of *diminishing marginal utility*, which is to say that the amount of utility received from a good decreases as the consumption of the good increases. For example, the first few dollars of income satisfy basic needs with a great increase in utility, while succeeding dollars satisfy lesser needs and bring less utility.
2. A system that maximizes utility also tends to reward people in proportion to such factors as their ability, effort, contribution or accomplishment, because rewarding in this way encourages people to develop their abilities and to contribute more to the welfare of society.

Mill's theory of justice. Mill believed that all persons possess a presumptive right to equal treatment unless the inequalities are justified by a social need. *Impartiality* (a part of justice closely related to equality) is an obligation that is part of the more general obligation to give everyone his or her right. Justice obliges individuals to treat others according to their rights, unless utility dictates otherwise. This obligation is implicit in the meaning of utility. Equality alone is not enough to account for justice, however, and so another criterion, such as utility, becomes necessary. Mill ultimately holds that equality is a part of utility although it can be overridden by other utility considerations.

The Egalitarian Theory of John Rawls

The contemporary American philosopher John Rawls has developed an egalitarian theory of justice that embodies the Kantian conception of equality and offers an alternative to utilitarianism. Rawls's theory focuses on *social justice*, which he regards as a feature of a well-ordered society. In such a society, free and equal persons are able to purse their interests in harmony because of institutions that assign rights and duties and distribute the benefits and burdens of mutual cooperation. Rawls's aim is not to develop the institutions of a well-ordered society but to determine the principles that would be used to evaluate the possibilities. And his method is to ask what principles a rationally self-interested person might agree to if he or she were to choose these principles in an *original position* behind a *veil of ignorance*. The original position is a hypothetical pre-contract situation similar to the state of nature in Locke's theory. The veil of ignorance requires that individuals choose the principles of justice without knowing any facts about their stations in life, such as social status, natural ability, intelligence, strength, race, and sex.

The principles of justice. Rawls acknowledges three principles of justice—the principle of equal liberty, the difference principle, and the principle of equal opportunity.

1. The *principle of equal liberty* holds that each person has an equal right to the most extensive set of basic liberties that are compatible with a system of liberty for all.
2. The *difference principle* allows an exception to the principle of equal liberty if some unequal arrangement benefits the least well-off person. That is, an unequal allocation is considered just if the worst-off person is better-off with the new distribution than the worst-off person under any other distribution.
3. The *principle of equal opportunity* provides that all public offices and employment positions be made available to everyone. Society should strive to offer all of its members an equal opportunity to fill positions through the elimination of differences caused by accidents of birth or social condition. Natural differences should be used for the benefit of all.

The basis for the first principle is that an equal share is the most that any person could reasonably expect considering the requirement for unanimous agreement in the original position. The second principle recognizes that a rational, impartial person would make an exception to the first principle and accept less than an equal share if everyone would be better off as a result of the inequality. Rawls's concern for the least advantaged is due to *maximin*, which is a rule of rational choice drawn from game theory according to which it is rational to maximize the minimum outcome when choosing between different alternatives. However, maximin is not the only rational choice of a person behind the veil of ignorance. One might use the principle of maximum average utility and assume some risk to increase his or her chances of becoming better-off. Whether Rawls's theory of justice is superior to utilitarianism depends, therefore, on the acceptability of maximin as a rule of rational choice.

Utility and the Market System

The market system is characterized by (a) *private ownership* of resources; (b) *voluntary exchange*; and (c) the *profit motive*. In the market system, individuals trade with one another, exchanging things they own for other things they want in order to improve their lives. The market system is justified by the utilitarian argument that it produces the highest level of welfare for society and by the rights-based argument that it is the best protection for liberty, particularly with regard to private property.

Adam Smith's "invisible hand" argument. Adam Smith (1723-1790), in his work *An Inquiry into the Nature and Causes of the Wealth of Nations* (1776), explains how trading motivated by self-interest rather than altruism best promotes the welfare of society. Each individual in pursuit of personal gain is "led by an invisible hand to promote an end [the welfare of society] which was no part of his intention." This argument, as it has been developed in neoclassical economics, does not prove that free markets maximize utility, only that they are efficient. Additionally, the argument that free markets are efficient presupposes that individuals are *rational utility maximizers* and that markets are characterized by *perfect competition* and freedom from *externalities*.

The invisible hand argument is further weakened by the problems of *collective choice* and *public goods*. A collective choice is a single choice that is made for an entire society by aggregating a multitude of individual choices. The underlying assumption is that if individuals make choices that are rational for them (that is, that maximize their own welfare), then the resulting collective choice is rational for the whole of society (that is, the collective choice maximizes total welfare). The *prisoner's dilemma* is a graphic demonstration that rational individual choices do not necessarily result in rational collective choices. The problem of public goods is that a market economy has a bias toward private consumption that results in the underfunding of goods that can be enjoyed by everyone, such as roads and public parks. The lack of profit in public goods, which is caused in part by *free riders*, leads the market to ignore such goods and leave them to government.

Libertarian Justification of the Market System

Libertarianism is committed to individual liberty conceived as the right to own property and live free from the interference of others. The free market is justified as the economic system that best supports individual liberty. Both utilitarianism and libertarianism support a system of free markets, but when the promotion of utility conflicts with the protection of liberty, libertarians favor unregulated markets that protect liberty, while utilitarians prefer regulation in order to increase utility at the expense of liberty.

Nozick's entitlement theory. The contemporary philosopher Robert Nozick presents a libertarian statement of the theory of justice that he calls the *entitlement theory* in the book *Anarchy, State and Utopia* (1974). Nozick's principles of justice are *historical principles* that take into account the process by which a distribution came about rather than the *nonhistorical* or *end-state* principles (such as those in utilitarianism and Rawls's theory) that evaluate a distribution with regard to certain structural features at a given time. In addition, Nozick's principles of justice are not *patterned*, inasmuch as patterned principles evaluate a distribution according to the presence or absence of that feature. Nozick contends that any particular pattern of distribution can be maintained only by continuously interfering in people's lives and hence violating the right to liberty. This is the point of the argument about Wilt Chamberlain.

The entitlement theory states that "a distribution is just if everyone is entitled to the holdings they possess." An expression of the non-patterned entitlement theory in patterned form is, "From each as they choose, to each as they are chosen." People are entitled to their holdings if the holdings were obtained by one of the following three principles:

1. The principle of just transfer.
2. The principle of just original acquisition.
3. The principle of rectification.

The original acquisition of a holding is just as long as it does not violate anyone else's rights. (Note the discussion in the text of the Lockean Proviso.) Transfers are just as long as they result from purely voluntary exchanges, provided that all preceding transfers were just reaching back to a just original acquisition. However, a principle of rectification is necessary to correct injustices in transfers and original acquisitions.

Justice and free markets. The market system is just because it protects individual rights better than any other economic system. The point of justice, for Nozick, is to protect rights, not to promote human well-being or to achieve equality, and a largely unregulated free market system, with only the absolute minimum of government intervention, protects rights best. However, Nozick fails to support his major assumption that liberty, understood as the unhindered exercise of property rights, is a paramount value. In addition, not all restrictions of liberty are due to interference by the state; individuals are sometimes restricted by the choices of others. The conditions for just original acquisitions and just transfers are often absent, and most distributions have been affected at some point in time by forced takings which have never been rectified in accord with the principle of rectification.

CASE SUMMARIES

Case 4.1 Green Giant Runs for the Border

Green Giant once employed more than 1,000 people in a frozen vegetable packaging plant in Watsonville, California. Green Giant began laying off workers in Watsonville and hiring new employees at a facility in Irapuato, Mexico, partly in an unsuccessful attempt to avoid a takeover by Grand Met. Today Green Giant employs fewer than 150 workers in California and more than 850 in Mexico. The economic benefits to Green Giant include significant savings on wages (from $7.50 per hour or $15,600 per year for workers in California to $4.50 per day and $1,400 per year for workers in Mexico, for a total savings of $13,224 per worker). The jobs in Mexico are well-paying by local standards but barely provide a minimum standard of living. Most of the laid-off American workers received severance pay and retraining but have been unable to find other work. An increase in demand for American products in Mexico and cheaper prices for imported goods from Mexico have benefited the U.S. economy. Mexicans in Irapuato receive some benefits from the plant, but they are also harmed by such factors as higher food costs due to export-driven production and the lowering of the water table because of the plant's demand for water.

Discussion Questions

1. Is justice an issue in evaluating Green Giant's move to Mexico? What specific features of the case raise issues of justice?

2. Evaluate Green Giant's move in terms of the benefits and harms for everyone concerned. On the whole, has the welfare of the U.S. and Mexico taken together been increased?

3. What different groups are impacted by this move? What are the benefits and burdens to the different groups? Have some groups benefited while others have been harmed? If so, have the harmed groups been treated unjustly?

4. Should Rawls's principle that any change should benefit the least advantaged be applied in the evaluation of Green Giant's move to Mexico? If so, what is the result of applying this principle?

5. Does Green Giant have any obligation to consider the impact of a decision to move a plant from one area to another? Any harm done by their move is an externality. Who should pay the cost of this externality?

6. Suppose that Green Giant had moved the plant from California to Texas, instead of to Mexico. Would this difference matter in evaluating the company's decision?

Case Objectives

The Green Giant example is a complex case that allows students to analyze how a corporation's actions cause a variety of benefits and harms that are unevenly distributed across diverse groups. The fact that the groups are in two different countries with different levels of economic development introduces an international element. The main objective in teaching the case is to determine which principle of justice should be used to evaluate Green Giant's decision to move to Mexico. Economic reasoning accords largely with a utilitarian analysis by holding that free trade benefits most groups in the long run. But what, if anything, is owed to groups that are not benefited at all and to groups that are harmed in the short run? The case also provides a good introduction to the issues of free trade and protectionism that occur in the debate over NAFTA, as well as the concept of corporate responsibility and its application in international business. A 20-minute video, "Your Job or Mine? Green Giant's Decision to Move to Mexico," is available from the University of Michigan Graduate School of Business Administration. The producer of the video, LaRue Tone Hosmer, has written a dialog with economist Scott E. Masten (who appears in the video) titled "Ethics vs. Economics: The Issue of Free Trade with Mexico," *Journal of Business Ethics*, 14 (1995), 287-289. In the article, Hosmer criticizes economic reasoning from a Rawlsian perspective.

Case 4.2 What's Fair

An ethicist and an economist discuss the fairest way to handle a gasoline shortage that has caused prices to increase between five and eight cents a gallon. The ethicist sees the free market as unfair in a shortage because it imposes an undue burden on the poor and increases inequality. The economist defends the fairness of a market distribution of resources and claims that the real problem is the unequal distribution of income and wealth. The ethicist recommends rationing gasoline through a coupon system. The economist points out, and the ethicist agrees, that the coupon holder should be allowed to trade the coupons in a free market, but the economist argues that such an arrangement is no different from a tax that is returned to the consumer as a coupon, except for the added administrative costs.

Discussion Questions

1. Do you agree with the ethicist that a shortage presents an exception to the claim that a free market generally sets prices fairly? What is unfair about the market price of goods in short supply? (Consider that we do not regard the high price of caviar as an ethical problem.)

2. Should holders of coupons be allowed to trade them on an open market? Would rationing lead to a fairer distribution if trading were not allowed? But would a prohibition against trading produce other kinds of unfairness?

3. Do you agree with the ethicist that the root of the problem is the market's distribution of resources or with the economist that the problem lies with the unequal distribution of income and wealth?

4. If a shortage unjustly increases the gap between the poor and the rich, would the government be entitled to tax the rich and give the money to the poor to offset this increase? Is this not what a rationing system would do, except that instead of being taxed, the rich would pay the poor directly by buying their coupons?

5. If market pricing is used, should gasoline producers be permitted to keep their "windfall" profits, or should it be taxed away? Would a windfall profits tax be an unjustified interference in a free market?

Case Objectives

"What's Fair" provides a test case for the justification of a free market and for evaluating solutions to one kind of market failure. Along with the Green Giant case, it provides an opportunity to compare economic and ethical reasoning and to discover how fairness can be achieved in a free market economy. In particular, this case asks whether achieving fairness is a job for the market alone or whether government plays a crucial role. Both the economist and the ethicist argue mainly from utilitarian grounds, but Nozickians considerations arise in deciding whether to allow a free market in coupons, because a prohibition on trading would illustrate Nozick's point in the Wilt Chamberlain example that maintaining any desired distribution would require constant interference in people's lives.

Case 4.3 Executive Compensation

Michael Eisner received $203 million as CEO of Walt Disney Company in 1993. In 1994, the highest paid executive earned $25.9 million, 25 executives were paid over $10 million, and the average total compensation for CEOs was $2.8 million. In the U.S., CEOs are paid ten to twelve times more than their counterparts in Japan and Europe, and they earn 25 times (100 times in *Fortune* 500 companies) the average pay for manufacturing employees. Critics charge that CEOs tend to receive their significant paychecks in good times and in bad, and even when they cause misery to laid-off employees. If CEO pay is based on the same factors as the pay of employees—such as responsibility, knowledge, skill, effort, and accomplishment—then higher pay might be justified, but studies indicated that these factors account for no more than 40 percent of CEO pay. Others argue, however, that the high salaries are needed to attract the best and the brightest to the field of management and that by this standard salaries are not too high but too low.

Discussion Questions

1. Are CEOs really overpaid, or is the public perception distorted by highly publicized instances of a few highly paid individuals?

2. How should executive pay be determined? Should executive pay be determined by the same factors that determine the pay of other employees, and if so, what are those factors? If wages are determined by market forces, is there a "market for CEOs?" If so, should that market not be allowed to work?

3. Are comparisons with CEO pay in Japan and Europe fair, or are there significant differences that ought to be considered?

4. Graef Crystal's studies suggest that highly paid sports and entertainment figures are less overpaid than CEOs. Do you agree with this conclusion?

Case Objectives

The case allows students to apply the principles of justice to a highly controversial, well-publicized topic. Executive compensation strikes many people as unfair, if not outrageous, but few are prepared to say why it is unfair or what would be fair. The case easily leads into a discussion of how pay should be set overall. Most people would apply either an Aristotelian principle of proportionality or a market mechanism to the determination of wages, and by either standard very high executive pay is difficult, but not impossible, to justify. Students may be divided on the implications of each of these standards. The comparison of executive compensation in the U.S. and the rest of the world can serve to illustrate the point that markets are influenced by cultural and other factors that are specific to a country. Executive compensation provides an especially good test case for Rawls's theory. Ask students whether they would choose principles of justice in Rawls's original position that would lead in practice to such high executive pay. *Business Week*, *Fortune*, and other business magazines publish stories annually on executive compensation for the past year, and these can be consulted for up-to-date data. The ABC News / Prentice Hall Video Library contains an eight minute Nightline report entitled "The U.S.'s Overpaid Executives."

TEACHING STRATEGIES

1. Discuss the fair distribution of a box of books on different subjects. Students will readily agree that the books should be in the hands of those who value them the most. For example, a book on gardening should go to an avid gardener. This exercise supports a utilitarian conception of justice. Then ask how a hypothetical distributor could know who values each book the most. This question illustrates the informational problems of utilitarian calculation, but this problem could be overcome by auctioning off each book (assuming that each person started the auction with the same amount of money). Finally, ask whether the same end could not be achieved by giving one book to each person and allowing him or her to trade. Through this exercise, students come to see the market as a mechanism for achieving a utilitarian end.

2. The exercise described above lends itself to many variations. First, suppose that someone cleverly trades and corners the market on all gardening books, so that avid gardeners have to pay high prices. Should the trader be rewarded for her cleverness or regarded as an economic parasite? Second, ask whether grades in the course should be given in the same way. Should high grades go to those who value them most? Should grades be auctioned off? This variation shows that a just distribution depends on the good involved, so that a fair distribution of medical care is different from a fair distribution of yachts.

3. The text treatment of the conditions for Adam Smith's "invisible hand" argument leads easily into a discussion of market failures and the remedies for them. Many business ethics problems result from market failures, especially those due to externalities and collective choice. The main remedies for market failures are government regulations and changes in the marketplace. Thus, an instructor can ask students whether pollution (which is an externality) is really a problem of ethics or merely a matter of getting the right mix of regulation (a governmental problem) and market reforms (an economic problem). In short, what is the *ethical* problem with pollution?

4. Free-riding is an important concept that is relevant to the analysis of many business ethics problems. So it may be worthwhile for an instructor to devote some time to showing how people who free-ride are acting unfairly by benefiting from the cooperation of others while refusing to cooperate themselves. Ask for instances of free-riding. For example, bribery, insider trading, and deceptive advertising are all instances of free-riding insofar as the effectiveness of these practices depends on others not engaging in them. The fact that many countries in Europe have voluntary fare systems on public transportation, which rely on people not to free-ride (literally), often provokes spirited student discussion about the conditions for such a system and the feasibility of a European-style system in the United States.

KEY TERMS AND CONCEPTS

basic liberties
bounded rationality
capitalist economy
collective choice
comparative justice
compensatory justice
convergence of utility and justice
desert
difference principle
differentiated products
diminishing marginal utility
distributive justice
economic man
economic justice
egalitarianism
end-state principles
entitlement theory
equality
external efficiency
externalities
fair
free market
free riders
historical principles
impartiality
imperfect procedural justice
internal efficiency
invisible hand

just original acquisition
just procedures
just transfer
justice
justifying features
least advantaged
legal justice
libertarianism
liberty
material goods
maximin
monopolies
moral equilibrium
necessary condition
neoclassical economics
noncomparative justice
nonmaterial goods
nonpatterned principles of justice
oligopolies
original position
particular justice
patterned principles of justice
perfect competition
perfect procedural justice
political justice
primary goods
principle of equal opportunity
principle of proportionate equality

principle of equal liberty

principle of justice

prisoners' dilemma

private ownership

problem of public goods

profit motive

pure procedural justice

rational

rectification

relevant differences

retributive justice

satisficing

social justice

state of nature

sufficient condition

supply and demand

transaction costs

universal justice

utility

veil of ignorance

voluntary exchange

CHAPTER FIVE

WHISTLE-BLOWING

CHAPTER SUMMARY

Chapter 5 defines whistle-blowing, discusses whether it is ever justified, and outlines the necessary elements for justified whistle-blowing. It additionally reviews the legal protection afforded whistle-blowers, compares the arguments for and against whistle-blower protection, and concludes with a discussion of corporate whistle-blowing policies.

CHAPTER OVERVIEW

Introduction

The term *whistle-blower* was initially used to describe government employees who went public with complaints of corruption or mismanagement but it is now applied to employees in the private sector as well. Whistle-blowing is ethically problematic because it involves a conflict between an employee's obligation to his or her company and a general obligation to the public. Employees are required not only to do the work they are assigned but also to be loyal to their employer, preserve the confidentiality of company information, and work in the best interest of the company. Deciding when whistle-blowing is morally justified and when it is not requires a balancing of many different obligations.

What is Whistle-Blowing?

Whistle-blowing is the voluntary release of non-public information, as a moral protest, by a member or former member of an organization to an appropriate audience outside the normal channels of communication regarding illegal and/or immoral conduct in the organization that is opposed to the public interest. The key points in this definition are:

1. A whistle-blower is a member or former member of an organization and not an outsider.
2. The information that is revealed by the whistle-blower is non-public information and not already-known facts.
3. The information concerns some significant misconduct by the organization or some of its members.
4. The information is revealed outside of the normal channels of corporate communication within an organization.
5. The information is revealed voluntarily and not by a legal mandate.
6. The information is revealed as a *moral protest* in order to correct some perceived wrong.

The Justification of Whistle-Blowing

Whistle-blowing pits an employee's loyalty to the organization against his or her loyalty to the public interest. The justification of whistle-blowing therefore requires an understanding of the duty of loyalty that an employee owes an employer.

The loyal agent argument against whistle-blowing. An employee is an *agent* of his or her employer. An agent is a person engaged to act in the interest of another person, who is known as the *principal*. Employees are legally agents of their employers. As agents, they are obligated to work as directed, to protect confidential information, and, in general, to act in the principal's best interest. Although the whistle-blower might appear to be a disloyal agent, the obligations of an agent's loyalty has limits. Whistle-blowing, therefore, is not incompatible with being a loyal agent. Two limits on the obligation of agents are especially important.

1. An agent has an obligation to obey only *reasonable* directives of the principal, and so an agent cannot be required to do anything illegal or immoral.
2. The obligations of an agent are confined to the needs of the relationship. Thus, an employee is not obligated to do anything that falls outside the scope of his or her employment.

The meaning of loyalty. The law of agency aside, whistle-blowing is not always an act of disloyalty in the ordinary meaning of the word. If loyalty is viewed as a commitment to the true interests or goals of an organization, rather than merely the following of orders, then many whistle-blowers are loyal employees. Sociological studies have shown that whistle-blowers are often loyal employees who choose to expose wrongdoing in the belief that they are doing their job and acting in the best interest of the company. In the book *Exit, Voice, and Loyalty*, Albert O. Hirschman holds that speaking out (voice) and leaving (exit) are the main options for dissatisfied organization members and that those who exercise the voice option are generally more loyal than those who decide to exit.

Conditions for Justified Whistle-Blowing

The following questions should be considered when deciding whether or not to blow the whistle.

1. Is the situation of sufficient moral importance to justify whistle-blowing? How serious is the potential harm compared to the possible benefits? To what extent is the harm a predictable and direct result of the protested activity? How imminent is the harm?
2. Do you have all the facts and have you properly understood their significance? Whistle-blowers must support allegations with adequate evidence and not draw conclusions about matters beyond their expertise.
3. Have all internal channels and steps short of whistle-blowing been exhausted? Most organizations require employees to address concerns with an immediate superior or through internal channels of communication.
4. What is the best way to blow the whistle? To whom should the information be revealed? How much information should be revealed? Blowing the whistle in a responsible manner avoids charges of being merely a disgruntled employee.
5. What is my responsibility in view of my role within the organization? An employee's position in the organization may increase or decrease an obligation to blow the whistle.

6. *What are the chances for success?* An employee should only blow the whistle when there is a reasonable chance to achieve some public good.

Is There a Right to Blow the Whistle?

Few laws exist to protect whistle-blowers from the retaliation of others, but there is increasing pressure for greater legal protection.

Existing legal protection. The *Civil Service Reform Act* of 1978 prohibits retaliation against federal employees who report waste and corruption in government. The *Merit System Protection Board* was set up by this act to receive and act on complaints of retaliation. The *Whistle-blower Protection Act* of 1989 further strengthens this protection with the creation of the *Office of Special Counsel* for processing whistle-blower reports. Anti-retaliation provisions in various pieces of federal legislation protect whistle-blowers in both the private and public sectors, and some statutes even encourage whistle-blowing in fraud cases by awarding a percentage of the funds recovered. More than 35 states have laws that protect whistle-blowers (although most of these apply only to government employees), and many state courts are limiting the grounds on which employees may be fired.

Arguments for and against whistle-blower protection. The main argument in favor of whistle-blower protection is that whistle-blowing benefits society through the exposure of illegal activity, waste, and mismanagement and this benefit can be achieved only if whistle-blowers are able to come forward without fear of retaliation. Government employees and private employers who do extensive work for the federal government have a First Amendment right to freedom of speech and so should be protected from retaliation for blowing the whistle. Although whistle-blowers in the *private sector* do not have a legal right to free speech in employment, this might be considered a *moral right* that requires legal protection. Finally, some argue that employees ought to have a right to act in accordance with one's own conscience.

One argument against legal protection for whistle-blowers is that a law that recognizes whistle-blowing as a right is open to abuse. Disgruntled employees might use whistle-blowing to protest company decisions, get back at employers, cover up their own incompetence or even protect themselves against dismissal. Legislation to protect whistle-blowers infringes on the traditional right of employers to conduct business as they see fit, and it creates more regulation to impede the efficient operation of business. An increase in litigation increases a company's costs and hurts the cooperative spirit needed for working relationships. Finally, it is difficult to devise an adequate legal remedy for whistle-blowers who are dismissed.

Developing a Company Whistle-Blowing Policy

An effective whistle-blowing policy enables a company to address misconduct internally and avoid embarrassing public disclosure. An effective policy ensures that reports are properly investigated, appropriate action is taken, and retaliation will not occur. Companies can benefit from a whistle-blowing policy by learning about problems early and taking corrective action. An effective whistle-blowing policy affirms a company's commitment to maintaining an ethical corporate climate. One danger connected with a whistle-blowing policy is that it can create an environment of mistrust and uncertainty.

41

Components of a whistle-blowing policy. A well-designed whistle-blowing policy should include the following:

1. An effectively communicated statement of responsibility.
2. A clearly-defined procedure for reporting.
3. Trained personnel to receive and investigate reports.
4. A commitment to take appropriate action.
5. A guarantee against retaliation.

CASE SUMMARIES

Case 5.1 Two Whistle-Blowers

Chuck Atchinson

Chuck Atchinson was a quality control inspector for Brown & Root, a construction company that was building a nuclear plant in Texas. Atchinson reported his company's failure to observe safety regulations to the government after he was unable to get his superiors to address his concerns. He was fired from his job soon after on the grounds of poor performance as a safety inspector. While testifying before government regulators, Atchinson received several threatening phone calls, and afterwards, he had difficulty finding work in his field. Atchinson and his family suffered financial and social loss as a result of his whistle-blowing.

Joseph Rose

Joseph Rose, an in-house attorney for the Associated Milk Producers Incorporated (AMPI), discovered that AMPI had made illegal political contributions to the Nixon re-election campaign. The confidentiality of his attorney-client relationship precluded him from releasing the information, but he advised the president of AMPI of the discovery and declared that he would no longer approve payments. He was prevented from presenting evidence to the board of directors and dismissed. AMPI then began slandering Rose in an effort to destroy his credibility in case he went public with his knowledge. As a result of Rose's testimony in court, AMPI was fined $35,000 and forced to pay $2.9 million in back taxes, and two executives were convicted of making illegal political contributions.

Discussion Questions

1. Did Chuck Atchinson and Joseph Rose do the right thing? What specific factors serve to justify their acts of whistle-blowing? Were their acts morally required? That is, would they have been acting wrongly had they not blown the whistle?
2. Were Atchinson and Rose loyal or disloyal employees? What exactly would a loyal employee do in their situations? Would they have been loyal employees if they had kept quiet?
3. How do the *roles* that Atchinson and Rose had in their companies bear on the justification of their actions? Does the fact that Atchinson was a quality control inspector and Rose a lawyer increase or decrease their responsibility to report wrongdoing?

42

4. Even if Atchinson and Rose acted correctly, were their employers within *their* rights to fire these two employees?

5. What could Brown & Root and AMPI do to avoid similar situations in the future? Should these companies seek to silence employees more effectively or encourage them to use internal lines of communication?

6. Should Atchinson and Rose be protected by law from the retaliation they suffered? Could a whistle-blower protection law be effective in such cases?

Case Objectives

The cases of Chuck Atchinson and Joseph Rose introduce various aspects of whistle-blowing. First, they serve as illustrations and test cases for the definition of whistle-blowing. The meaning of loyalty and the conflict that exists between loyalty to the company and loyalty to the public are seen in both cases. Each displays the choice of means for blowing the whistle and the retaliation that whistle-blowers often encounter. These cases can also be used to introduce the conditions for justified whistle-blowing and the need for legal protection for whistle-blowers. For fuller accounts of both cases, see Myron Peretz Glazer and Penina Migdal Glazer, *The Whistleblowers: Exposing Corruption in Government and Industry* (New York: Basic Books, 1989).

Case 5.2 A Whistle-Blower Accepts a "Deal"

The head of a corporate audit for a major pharmaceutical company discovered that "double books" had been kept on the research for a new drug and that the original data showed the drug failing every required test. Following the procedure in the company's own whistle-blowing policy, he submitted a report stating only documented facts. The auditor was summoned to meet with the directors, who offered him a "deal." They promised that if the auditor would keep quiet about the falsification, the company would never market the drug. The auditor agreed and the directors kept their promise. However, corporate policy was changed to prohibit the auditor from having ready access to company records. In addition, individual departments were given the authority to stop internal audits and to review the audit reports before they are submitted. The auditor wonders whether he should have accepted that "deal."

Discussion Questions

1. Was the auditor offered a *good* "deal?" Should he have accepted? What were his alternatives?

2. Was anyone hurt by the deal? (Consider both the short term and the long term consequences.)

3. Was the board of directors acting responsibly in making the deal? Were they acting responsibly when they subsequently changed the audit procedures?

4. Was the auditor actually blowing the whistle, given that he was following company policy? What should he have done if the policy had not been in place?

5. On the whole, did the policy serve the company well? The employee? The public?

Case Objectives

This case focuses on a little examined aspect of whistle-blowing, namely what constitutes a satisfactory outcome. Any potential whistle-blower should ask, what result am I trying to achieve?

A whistle-blower may also have to make a decision about whether the result has been achieved or whether further action is called for. The case additionally allows for a comparison between internal whistle-blowing and external whistle-blowing. The consequences from this case of internal whistle-blowing should be compared and contrasted with the probable consequences had the auditor blown the whistle with the FDA.

Case 5.3 Better Late Than Never?

Rockland International has a seven year old whistle-blowing policy that requires employees to report any suspicions of unethical or illegal conduct and assures employees that they will not suffer any adverse consequences from complying with the policy. Art Holmes called Rockland's whistle-blowing hotline and presented copies of canceled checks and invoices as evidence that his immediate supervisor, the head of the purchasing department, was involved in a kickback scheme with a supplier. The purchasing department head resigned after making restitution. The entire company knew of the scheme and of Holmes' role in uncovering it. However, the copies of the checks and invoices presented by Holmes were over a year old, and Holmes's job is due to be eliminated. Ken Dryden, the company investigator, wonders whether Holmes blew the whistle in an attempt to protect his job.

Discussion Questions

1. Is Holmes abusing the whistle-blowing policy? If Holmes has evidence of genuine wrongdoing and reveals it in accord with the policy, why should his motive matter?
2. Any policy can be abused. So is the problem in this case with the formulation of the policy or with the implementation? If the problem is the formulation, how should the policy be changed?
3. Given the potential for abuse, is a whistle-blowing policy worth the risks? What are the advantages of a company whistle-blowing policy? On the whole, do these advantages outweigh the risks?
4. What should Dryden do in this situation? Would the policy be violated if Holmes were terminated because of the previously planned reductions? Would trust in the policy be seriously eroded if Holmes were terminated?

Case Objectives

This case highlights an important objection to company whistle-blowing policies. Any policy must protect employees against retaliation for following the procedures stated in the policy. However, this protection invites employees to take out "anti-dismissal insurance" by saving up information about wrongdoing and revealing it when their jobs are endangered. The case presents a whistle-blowing policy for evaluation and asks students how this possible abuse can be avoided. The instructor may choose to focus on how the policy should have been formulated initially or on how the manager should respond now that a flaw in the policy has been revealed.

TEACHING STRATEGIES

1. The general concept of agency and the specific obligations of agents are highly relevant to business ethics, and the chapter on whistle-blowing provides a good opportunity to introduce this important material. Instructors who are unfamiliar with the law of agency may want to consult any standard text on business law. For the bearing of principal-agent analysis on business ethics, a useful volume is Norman E. Bowie and R. Edward Freeman, eds., *Ethics and Agency Theory* (New York: Oxford University Press, 1992). The agency relation is also an important feature of professionals, and so the instructors may want to explore (1) the obligations of professionals in business, such as accountants, and (2) the similarities and differences between professional and nonprofessional employees.

2. In addition to the cases in the text, the following are recommended. (1) Sally Seymour, "The Case of the Willful Whistle-Blower" in *Cases in Ethics and the Conduct of Business*. (2) The video "The Whistleblower," which is one of three cases in *Business Ethics*. A Teaching Note on "The Whistleblower" is available from the Harvard Business School. "The Whistleblower" is a three-part video that allows the instructor to stop at crucial points in the case and discuss the issues as the case unfolds.

3. Whistle-blowers often receive extensive press coverage. Assign students, individually or in groups, to collect a number of sample news stories and to draw some generalizations from them. Ask them to consider, for example, whether incidents of whistle-blowing differ according to the industry or whether whistle-blowers exhibit any similar features.

4. Ask groups of students to develop a specific whistle-blowing policy for a hypothetical company. As a variant, specify a different industry for each group, so that one writes a policy for, say, a retail merchandiser, and another for a manufacturing company, and seek to determine whether the policies differ as a result.

KEY TERMS AND CONCEPTS

agent
Civil Service Reform Act of 1978
duty of loyalty to the public
duty of loyalty to the organization
exit and voice
external whistle-blowing
internal whistle-blowing
loyal agent argument
loyalty
Merit System Protection Board
moral protest
normal channels of communication
ombudsman
principal
retaliation
sounding the alarm
whistle-blower
Whistle-blower Protection Act of 1989

CHAPTER SIX

TRADE SECRETS AND CONFLICT OF INTEREST

CHAPTER SUMMARY

All businesses seek to protect certain valuable information, but what information do they have a *right* to keep secret? Moreover, what are the ethical obligations of current and former employees to protect such information and not use it to their own advantage? Companies also have an obligation to respect the secrets of their competitors, but they have a right to use any information that they can legitimately acquire. This chapter examines the three main grounds for justifying trade secret protection, namely property rights, fair competition, and confidentiality, and explores the ethics of competitor intelligence gathering. The chapter also discusses the concept of conflict of interest in order to determine what is ethically objectionable about such conflicts and to classify the various types of conflict of interest. One argument against insider trading is that it constitutes a conflict of interest, and so the ethical objections to insider trading are considered.

CHAPTER OVERVIEW

Introduction

A trade secret is any formula, pattern, device or compilation of information used in one's business to give it an advantage over competitors. Some examples of trade secrets include the chemical composition of a product, the design of a machine, the details of a manufacturing process, and the results of marketing surveys. Trade secrets also involve intellectual property protected by patents, copyrights, and trademarks. Confidential business information, on the other hand, is information kept secret but not actually used to produce anything. An example would be the salary of an employee.

Six factors can be used to determine whether information is protectable as a trade secret:

1. The extent to which the information is known outside the business.
2. The degree to which it is known by employees and others involved in the business.
3. The measures required to guard the secrecy of the information.
4. The value of the information to the business and its competitors.
5. The amount of effort required to develop the information.
6. The ease with which the information can be acquired or duplicated by others.

Trade Secrets as Property

Trade secrets are commonly regarded as intellectual property belonging to an owner. In the case of patents, copyrights, and trademarks, the owner has the right of exclusive use and the right to sell, license, or otherwise assign ownership to others. These rights do not depend on keeping the information secret. Ownership of a trade secret merely confers protection against having the secret misappropriated by others, and others are free to use the information once it becomes commonly known. The question of who owns information is complicated when an inventor is employed by the manufacturer of the product. If an inventor develops an idea while performing unrelated work for his or her employer and conducts experiments on personal time, then it seems only right that he or she be recognized as the sole owner. But if the individual is specifically hired as an inventor to develop a new product or process, then some or all the ownership rights should belong to the employer. The rights of employers in such cases are expressed by the "hired-to-invent" test and the "shop right" concept.

A key court case for understanding the rights of employees is *Wexler v. Greenberg*. Alvin Greenberg was a chief chemist for the Buckingham Wax Company who analyzed the products of competitors in order to develop new formulas. After eight years, he left Buckingham Wax Company to join Brite Products, which had previously purchased exclusively from Buckingham. With the formulas that Greenberg developed while working for Buckingham, Brite was now able to produce its own waxes and polishes, whereupon Buckingham sued to prevent Greenberg and his new employer from using the formulas. In *Wexler v. Greenberg*, the court ruled that information is protectable as a trade secret only as long as (a) the information is a genuine trade secret and (b) the user of the information has violated some legal obligation. The court found that the formulas were not significant discoveries on Greenberg's part but were merely the result of routine applications of his skill as a chemist. Thus, they are not genuine trade secrets. In addition, Greenberg developed the formulas himself, and so he had a right to use them in his work for a new employer. The owner of a secret has a right to prevent its use by competitors when the information is obtained by theft, bribery, espionage, or other illegal means or when an employee violates an obligation of confidentiality, but no such legal obligations were violated in this case.

Source of property rights. Locke's political philosophy provides one source of support from the idea that information is a form of property. Locke held that we come to own property as the result of our own labor, so that a farmer who clears land and a writer who writes a novel both have ownership rights in the products of their labor. There are utilitarian reasons for recognizing intellectual property rights. One is that society benefits from the willingness of companies to innovate, but without the legal protection provided by patent and trade secret laws, companies would have less incentive to make investments in research and development. Another is that patent and copyright laws encourage a free flow of information, which leads to additional benefits. There are also drawbacks to such legal protection. A patent confers a legal monopoly for a fixed number of years, which raises the price that the public pays for patented products during that time. Trade secrets permit a monopoly to exist as long as a company succeeds in keeping key information out of the hands of its competitors. And the owner of copyrighted material can prevent the wide dissemination of important information.

Many companies attempt to clarify the ownership of patentable ideas by requiring employees to sign an agreement whereby they turn over all patent rights to the employer. Such agreements are morally objectionable, however, when they give companies a claim on discoveries that fall outside the scope of an employee's responsibilities. This is a difficult area for the law because the contributions of employers and employees are so often hard to disentangle. The law in the U.S. has tended to favor employers.

Fair Competition

Even when information is not easily classifiable as property and there is no contract barring disclosure or use of the information, it may still be protected on the grounds of fair competition. Employees have a right to seek new employment and to compete with a former employer. In the *Wexler* case, the court considered the fact that any post-employment restraint reduces the economic mobility of employees and limits their freedom to choose their livelihood. The case *Associated Press v. International News Service* (1918) is relevant here. The Associated Press complained that the International News Service was rewriting its stories and selling them to competing newspapers. The International News Service argued that although the specific wording of a news story can be regarded as property, the content itself cannot belong to anyone. Moreover, it asserted that it had not breached any contract or acquired the information by any other unlawful means. Justice Brandeis, in the minority opinion, sided with the International News Service, noting that the general rule of law is that the noblest of intellectual productions becomes, after voluntary communication to others, free for common use. But the majority sided with the Associated Press, arguing that the case ought to be decided not on the grounds of property rights but on grounds of fair competition. The International News Service was judged to be "endeavoring to reap where it has not sown." Specifically, the court rules that if a company has acquired something at substantial cost in order to earn a profit, a competitor has no right to misappropriate it for the purpose of his own profit.

Noncompetition agreements. Many companies require employees to sign non-competition agreements that typically restrict employees from working for a competitor or within a given geographical territory for a certain period of time after leaving a company. There is little justification for restricting employees in this way, and noncompete agreements function almost entirely for the benefit of the employer. Accordingly, the courts have generally imposed restrictions on them. Noncompetition agreements must:

1. Serve to protect legitimate business interests.
2. Not be more restrictive than that which is required for the protection of these legitimate interests.
3. Not impose an undue hardship on the ability of an employee to secure employment.
4. Not be injurious to the public.

In determining whether restrictions on non-competition agreements undermine the legitimate interests of an employer, the courts have generally considered the time period specified, the geographical area involved, and the kind of work that is excluded.

The Confidentiality Argument

The principal-agent relationship generally obliges agents to keep confidential any information that is revealed by a principal. The obligation of confidentiality continues to exist after an employee has left one job for another. Companies may also have an obligation of confidentiality when they enter into various relations with each other. Thus, a company that inveigles trade secrets from another company under the guise of negotiating a licensing agreement or a merger might be charged with a breach of confidentiality. Many companies seek to protect information by requiring employees to sign confidentiality agreements, but Michael Baram contends that such measures rarely preserve either the secrecy of company information or the liberty of employees. Instead of requiring confidentiality agreements, he suggests that companies secure the legal protection of patents, copyrights, and trademarks whenever possible, segment information so that fewer people know the full scope of a trade secret, and use pension supplements and post-employment consulting contracts to discourage employees from finding competitive employment. In general, the best way to protect trade secrets is to foster good employee relations.

Competitor Intelligence Gathering

The systematic collection and analysis of competitor intelligence has become an accepted and even essential business practice, but there are also ethical and legal limits that companies ignore at their peril. These limits on competitor intelligence gathering are generally concerned with the methods used to acquire the information. There are four means of unethical competitor intelligence gathering:

1. Theft and receipt of unsolicited information.
2. Misrepresentation.
3. Improper influence.
4. Covert surveillance.

Each of these means violates some important moral consideration. Thus, misrepresentation is a form of deception, improper influence may induce an employee to breach a duty of confidentiality, and covert surveillance may violate a company's right to privacy. Determining the exact limits for each means is often difficult.

Conflict of Interest

Virtually all corporate codes of ethics address conflict of interest, since it interferes with an employee's ability to act in the best interests of an employer. A conflict of interest may result from accepting gifts or lavish entertainment from customers or suppliers, or from investing in customers, suppliers, or competitors. However, conflict of interest does not ordinarily rule out an employee's pursuit of unrelated business opportunities or his or her participation in community and political affairs. Perhaps no other business ethics concept is so elusive and subject to dispute.

What is conflict of interest? A conflict of interest may be defined precisely as a conflict that occurs when a personal interest interferes with a person's acting so as to promote the interest of another *when the person has an obligation to act in that other person's interest.* The italicized phrase reflects the point that a conflict of interest can arise only in certain kinds of relations, which are roughly those of an agent to a principal. This definition shows that a conflict of interest is not merely a conflict between the interests of agent and principal but a conflict between an agent's personal interest and his or her obligation to serve the principal. In addition, the personal interest must be substantial enough to interfere significantly with the agent's performance of the obligation towards the principal. Company codes of ethics and the codes of professionals make a number of important distinctions.

1. *Actual and potential conflicts of interest.* A conflict is *actual* when a personal interest leads a person to act against the interests of an employer or another person whose interests the person is obligated to serve. A situation constitutes a *potential* conflict of interest when there is the possibility

that an agent will fail to fulfill an obligation to act in the interests of the principal but the agent has not yet done so.

2. *Personal and impersonal conflicts of interest.* *Personal* conflicts are those where the agent has something to gain. An impersonal conflict arises when the agent is obligated to act in the interests of two different principals whose interests conflict. Thus, a lawyer or an accountant may have nothing to gain personally from favoring one client over the other but cannot fully serve both when their interests conflict.

3. *Individual and organizational conflict.* Like individuals, organizations can be agents and hence parties to conflicts of interest. For example, many large accounting firms provide management services to companies that they also audit. This dual role endangers the independence and objectivity of accountants. Banking houses and large law firms encounter similar challenges.

Kinds of conflict of interest. Conflicts of interest may arise in many kinds of situations. Four, in particular, may be distinguished:

1. *Biased judgment.* Biased judgment arises in situations where large gifts, bribes, kickbacks, and other inducements interfere with the obligation of an agent to use specialized knowledge on behalf of a principal.

2. *Direct competition.* This occurs when an employee engages in direct competition with his or her employer. It is ordinarily prohibited by companies even if it is disclosed and presents no danger of impairing the employee's judgment or diminishing his or her work performance.

3. *Misuse of position.* Misuse of position can occur even when an employee's personal interests have no effect on decisions made for the employer. Thus, a bank manager who refers loan customers to a family member in the contracting business misuses her position even though the referral has no affect on the loan decision.

4. *Violation of confidentiality.* This kind of conflict of interest occurs, for example, when an employee uses information gained in the course of employment for his or her advantage or a lawyer uses information gained from a client for personal business dealings.

The Ethics of Insider Trading

Insider trading is sometimes regarded as a conflict of interest, but the practice raises additional issues. Although insider trading is generally illegal, both the definition of the practice and the arguments against it are far from settled.

The definition of insider trading. Insider trading is commonly defined as trading in the stock of publicly held corporations on the basis of material, non-public information. In a landmark 1968 decision, executives of Texas Gulf Sulphur Company were found guilty of insider trading for investing heavily in their own company's stock after learning of the discovery of rich copper ore deposits in Canada. The rule for corporate insiders is: "reveal or refrain." Corporate executives are definitely "insiders," but some "outsiders" have also been charged with insider trading. In general, outsiders are barred from trading when they know or should know that the information has come from an insider. Thus, the rule for outsiders is: don't trade on information that is revealed in violation of a trust.

The arguments against insider trading. Two main rationales are used in support of a law against insider trading.

1. According to one argument, insider trading is a form of *theft*, since insiders who trade on material, nonpublic information are essentially stealing property that belongs to the corporation. This argument leads to a narrow definition because only corporate insiders or outsiders who bribe, steal or otherwise wrongfully acquire corporate secrets could be guilty of insider trading; someone who overhears a conversation or otherwise gains information legitimately would be free to trade. A weakness of this argument is that it may be difficult to determine who owns information or why a company should have a right to it. If companies own certain information, they should be able to give it to their employees or to favored investors, and even to trade on it themselves.

2. The second argument is that insider trading is *unfair*, which is to say that traders who use inside information have an unfair advantage over other investors. If insider trading were common, the market would be less efficient because of people's reluctance to trade. This argument leads to a broader definition that applies to anyone who trades on material, nonpublic information no matter how it is acquired. The main weakness of the fairness argument is that it is very difficult to determine what information ought to be revealed about a transaction. Moreover, some economists argue that the market would be more efficient without a law against insider trading. If insider trading were permitted, they claim, information would be registered in the market more quickly and at less cost. Supporters of the fairness argument claim that economic arguments about market efficiency look only at the cost of registering information in the market and not at other, adverse consequences.

CASE SUMMARIES

Case 6.1 The Aggressive Ad Agency

Rob Lebow, the director of corporate communications for Microsoft, received a flier from Neal Hill at Rossin Greenberg Seronick & Hill (RGS&H), a small New England advertising agency. The flier stressed the agency's familiarity with Lotus 1-2-3, which was the main competition for Microsoft's new spreadsheet program, Excel. RGS&H had recently hired two people who had worked on the Lotus account for another advertising agency, and so Lebow wondered whether RGS&H was offering Microsoft the skill and experience of these new employees or whether the agency was offering to sell confidential information that belonged to Lotus. Lebow had four options: he could ignore RGS&H's flier; he could return the flier with the reply, "Thanks but no thanks;" he could forward the flier to Lotus; or he could investigate the offer.

Discussion Questions

1. Which option should Lebow choose? What are the main arguments for and against each one?
2. What information could the new employees at RGS&H provide that would be of use to Microsoft? That is, why should Microsoft be interested at all?
3. How much of this information could be provided ethically? What distinguished the information that could be provided ethically from the information that could not be provided ethically?

4. What advantage could Microsoft gain by forwarding the flier to Lotus? Hint: should the treatment of confidential information in the advertising industry be of concern to Microsoft?

5. Did RGS&H really offer to sell confidential information? Was Neal Hill guilty of a crime or merely of poor judgment in his choice of words?

Case Objectives

This case illustrates the difficulty of distinguishing confidential information that a company has a right to protect and determining the limits of legitimate use of competitor intelligence. The main focus of the case is on the information possessed by the two new employees at RGS&H. The flier does not describe the information, but by speculating on what it might be, students can come to understand the competitive value of information. The instructor should press students to develop a principle for distinguishing information that can legitimately be provided to Microsoft and information that ought to be protected as confidential. The case also focuses on the decision that Rob Lebow had to make. Even if wrong for RGS&H to offer the information, would it be wrong for Microsoft to accept the offer? The outcome of the case is instructive. Lebow forwarded the flier to Lotus. Lotus promptly sued RGS&H for offering to sell trade secrets to a competitor, and the suit was settled out of court. Neal Hill apologized for the misunderstanding but insisted that he was offering only the expertise of his employees and not confidential information. At some point in the discussion, the instructor should reveal the outcome and ask why Microsoft would forward the flier to Lotus. Among the factors to consider are the threat to Microsoft's reputation if news of the offer became known in the industry and the danger to Microsoft if their own advertising agencies could not be trusted with confidential information. There is also an important management lesson: Neal Hill may have acted thoughtlessly and thereby damaged not only his own company but two (possibly innocent) employees.

Case 6.2 Three Trade Secret Disputes

Spies in the Sky

DuPont successfully sued when a competitor attempted to discover an unpatented process for producing methanol by hiring an aerial photographer to take photographs of a DuPont plant that was still under construction. However, a competitor intelligence firm, Research Source, Inc., provides clients with publicly available aerial photographs from government sources. Although portions of these photographs can be made to reveal details of companies' manufacturing facilities, this service is apparently legal.

Discussion Questions

1. What accounts for the different legal status of these two practices? What are the relevant difference between them, and why is this difference relevant?

Case Objectives

This case illustrates the distinction between spying and legitimate access to proprietary information. The main relevant difference between the two practices is that the information is in the public domain in one case and in the private domain in the other case. But why is this difference relevant? One possible answer to the question posed in the case is that companies should have a reasonable expectation of privacy and this right is violated when a competitor hires an aerial photographer for the purpose of gaining proprietary information. No similar right is violated when the government conducts aerial surveillance for legitimate purposes, and, in any event, a right to privacy does not extend to information in the public domain. Ask students to compare government aerial photographs with publicly available records, such as SEC filings, which companies examine to gain information about their competitors.

Mouldings, Inc.

Two women launched a line of plastic dessert molds in the shapes of animals and seasonal symbols. Since they discovered that the most popular filling for the molds was a dessert made from Kellogg's Rice Krispies, they proposed a joint promotion with Kellogg. When Kellogg expressed interest, the women sent some sample molds and a price list. They heard nothing more until they discovered that Kellogg awarded a contract for molds to another manufacturer. The women sued, claiming that Kellogg had stolen its idea. Kellogg countersued on the grounds that the women had infringed the Rice Krispies trademark in the recipes that were distributed with their molds.

Discussion Questions

1. Is the idea of dessert molds in the shape of animals and seasonal symbols sufficiently original to deserve legal protection?
2. Were the women entitled to assume that their idea, which was initially sent to Kellogg unsolicited, would not be appropriated by Kellogg? Does Kellogg have any obligation not to appropriate any ideas that are submitted to the company?
3. Did the women really infringe the Rice Krispies trademark?

Case Objectives

This case illustrates the difficulty of determining who owns ideas and what constitutes misappropriation. The women took no steps to protect their idea, and it could be argued that they were merely proposing to supply a standard item to Kellogg. On the other hand, companies have long misappropriated the ideas that inventors have brought to them. Does the willingness of companies to entertain ideas imply a guarantee against misappropriation? (Note: some companies avoid this problem by not receiving unsolicited ideas, so that they cannot be charged with misappropriation.)

Spaghetti Wars

Hunt-Wesson's research indicated a consumer demand for a thicker spaghetti sauce and the effectiveness of the slogan "Extra Thick and Zesty." Before the company could bring the new product to market, Ragu introduced its own new, thicker "Ragu Extra Thick and Zesty" spaghetti sauce. Hunt-Wesson sued Ragu for appropriating its ideas and suppressing competition by confusing consumers. Ragu claimed that the idea of a thicker sauce and Hunt-Wesson's accompanying slogan are not original and that meeting competition is simply good business.

1. Is the idea of a thick sauce or the slogan "Thick and Zesty" deserving of protection? Did Hunt-Wesson make an investment in the development of this new product? On what other grounds could Hunt-Wesson claim protection for the idea and the slogan?

2. If Ragu developed their product merely to counter Hunt-Wesson's entry into the prepared spaghetti sauce market, did they do anything wrong? Is this just good business, or is it an anticompetitive practice?

Case Objectives

This case bears on the fair competition argument for trade secret protection. The idea of a thick sauce and the slogan "Thick and Zesty" are not easily classified as property. Moreover, Ragu did not acquire advance information about the new product through any objectionable means. It is worth noting, however, that the value of the idea and the slogan are not attributable to the cost of creating them but to the cost of the research that verified the consumer demand for a thicker sauce and the effectiveness of "Thick and Zesty." Arguably, Ragu "stole" the results of Hunt-Wesson's market research. It could also be argued that the case is not about the protection of information at all but about anticompetitive marketing practices, and in fact the suit by Hunt-Wesson alleged violations of various antitrust laws. The appeals court decision, cited in a footnote in the text, did not resolve any substantive issues in the case but addressed only procedural matters and ordered the case to be retried.

Case 6.3 The Conflict of an Insurance Broker

As an insurance broker, Ashton & Ashton (A&A) seeks to obtain the best available insurance coverage for its clients. For this service, A&A charges clients a commission, which is a percentage of the amount of the premium, and the firm also receives a contingency payment from the insurance providers based on the volume of business. One of A&A's clients is a museum, which has a very tight operating budget. For many years, Haverford Insurance Company had offered the best policy for the museum and paid A&A an above average commission. The museum would be best served by continuing with Haverford, but another company, named Reliable, submits an unsolicited "low ball" bid that the museum might choose if it is presented to them. Should A&A present the bid to the museum and allow the client to make the choice, or should the firm present only the bids that would serve the client well? Complicating the decision is the fact that A&A would also benefit if the museum were to continue with Haverford, thus creating a potential conflict of interest.

Discussion Questions

1. Should A&A present the Reliable bid to the museum, knowing that the museum might be forced by financial pressure to accept it?

2. As an agent of the museum, A&A is obligated to act in the museum's best interest. What specifically does this obligation entail? Hint: compare the role of an insurance broker with the roles of physicians and lawyers, who are also obligated to act in the best interest of a patient or a client.

3. Does the compensation system for insurance brokers create the right incentives? Should the system be changed?

Case Objectives

This case illustrates conflicts of interest in the agent-principal relation as well as uncertainty about the obligations of agents. First, the obligation of an agent to act in the best interest of a principal does not provide a guide to action when the two parties disagree about what is in the principal's best interest. Whose judgment should prevail in such situations? Similar problems arise in medical and legal ethics, and a comparison with these problems can clarify but not resolve the dilemma faced by A&A. A physician, for example, is obligated to present all available therapies to a patient, and to do otherwise would be considered *paternalistic*. On the other hand, a physician must use professional judgment in determining the range of available therapies that are to be presented to a patient. Thus, students might be asked to compare the Reliable bid to a dubious therapy a physician might fear a patient would accept.

Second, even if accepting Haverford's bid is in the museum's best interest, the benefit to A&A creates a potential conflict of interest. The compensation system is part of the problem, and perhaps the system should be changed or at least revealed to all clients. However, A&A ought to be concerned about other factors, such as the firm's reputation, future relations with the museum and reputable insurers. Do these factors really create a conflict of interest? There is a "solution" to this case that satisfactorily addresses all of the ethical issues. A&A could present the Reliable bid to the museum with its candid evaluation but declare that the firm would no longer serve as the museum's insurance broker if the museum were to accept the Reliable bid.

TEACHING STRATEGIES

1. Software piracy provides an example of intellectual property with which students are familiar and on which they may have differing views, and so the topic serves well as a discussion starter. The topic also has an international dimension, especially in U.S.-Chinese trade relations, since developing countries generally argue for freer use of intellectual property. See Paul Steidlmeier, "The Moral Legitimacy of Intellectual Property Claims," *Journal of Business Ethics*, 12 (1993), 157-164. For a case on software piracy as well as vendor relations, see "Agrico, Inc.—A Software Dilemma" in *Cases in Ethics and the Conduct of Business*.

2. Ask one or more students to research the resources for competitor intelligence gathering. Students are often surprised at the spy techniques that are available and the extent of their use, especially by foreign competitors. Some instructors may want to discuss corporate policies on competitor intelligence gathering. A useful case on the development of such a policy is "Competitive Information Policy at Pratt & Whitney," Harvard Business School case 9-394-154.

3. An excellent video case on proprietary information and competing with one's employer is "Jeff Arnold: Project Administrator" in *A Matter of Judgment*. Jeff Arnold and his wife Laura discuss their dream of starting their own business by marketing a software program for a programmer who has approached Jeff at his place of employment. The video case permits the use of "What ifs" to explore the different conditions under which Jeff and Laura might ethically seize this opportunity.

4. Confidentiality and noncompetition agreements are contractual solutions to managerial problems. Ask students to brainstorm noncontractual, managerial solutions to each of these problems. For example, ask students to develop procedures and policies that promote the confidentiality of information. Some suggestions might include improving security in the workplace; securing the legal protection of patents, copyrights, and trademarks; segmenting information so that fewer people know the full scope of trade secrets; increasing pensions and post-employment consulting contracts; and recognizing employees for their contributions.

5. Ask students to find examples of conflicts of interest from their own work experience and the experience of parents, relatives, and friends. Alternatively, ask students to examine some corporate codes of ethics (most of which have a section on conflict of interest) and to list the specific conflict of interest situations that are described in the codes. For a fictional case on a conflict of interest policy that is based on an actual event, see "Steve Charles: Implementing a Conflict of Interest Policy" in *Cases in Ethics in the Conduct of Business*.

6. Insider trading usually provokes heated student discussion. Students are often surprised by the unsettled legal definition of insider trading and the ease with which unwary investors can run afoul of the law. As a exercise, present a list of hypothetical or actual scenarios and ask students to decide which constitute illegal insider trading. Although the landmark legal cases are discussed in the text, other scenarios can be developed from articles on insider trading that appear in the business press. The text discussion of R. Foster Winans can be supplement by the case "R. Foster Winans" in *Cases in Ethics and the Conduct of Business*. A twenty-minute video case on the temptation of an MBA student to engage in insider trading is "Legal Tender," produced by the Stanford Business School.

7. The definition of conflict of interest in the text has been criticized in several academic articles. Although the subject may be too abstract for a business course, instructors of courses with a more philosophical orientation might want to pursue these criticisms. See Michael Davis, "Conflict of Interest Revisited," *Business and Professional Ethics Journal*, 12(4) (1993), 21-41; with a reply by John R. Boatright, "Conflict of Interest: A Response to Michael Davis," *Business and Professional Ethics Journal*, 12(4) (1993), 43-46. See also Thomas Carson, "Conflicts of Interest," *Journal of Business Ethics*, 13 (1994), 387-404. Boatright's definition is developed in more detail in "Conflict of Interest: An Agency Analysis," in Norman E. Bowie and R. Edward Freeman, eds., *Ethics and Agency Theory* (New York: Oxford University Press, 1992), 187-203.

KEY TERMS AND CONCEPTS

actual/potential conflict of interest	improper influence
agent-principal relation	individual/organizational conflict of interest
Associated Press v. *International News Service*	insider trading
biased judgment	John Locke
bribery and extortion	misrepresentation
confidentiality	misuse of position
copyright	noncompetition agreement
covert surveillance	patent
direct competition	personal/impersonal conflict of interest

trade secret
trademark
Wexler v. *Greenberg*

CHAPTER SEVEN

PRIVACY

CHAPTER SUMMARY

Privacy is a value, indeed a right, that is fundamental to one's identity as a person. Issues about privacy arise for both employees and consumers. In the workplace, privacy is an issue primarily about the way that personal information is gathered and used by employers. All rights have limits, and the purpose of this chapter is to determine the limits to an employee's right to privacy. Three issues are examined with regard to privacy in the workplace: (1) What is privacy? (2) Why is privacy a value? (3) What does a right of employee privacy entail? Consumer privacy is at issue mainly in the handling of information that marketers gather, especially for purposes of direct mail advertising.

CHAPTER OVERVIEW

Introduction

Although privacy is an important value, we are obligated to provide a certain amount of personal information to others. However, there are limits beyond which business, government, and others are not entitled to go. One way to protect workers from abuses of corporate power is by recognizing their right to privacy. But finding the right balance between the rights of employers and employees in matters of privacy is difficult.

The Concept of Employee Privacy: Three Definitions

As an ethical concept, the definition of privacy is very elusive. According to Warren and Brandeis in a famous 1890 article, privacy is "the right to be left alone." This definition was slow to gain acceptance, but gradually most states followed New York State's lead in granting persons a right to be free from certain types of intrusion into their private lives. In *Griswold v. Connecticut* (1965)—which involved the use of contraceptives by married couples—the Supreme Court held that privacy is a right guaranteed by the Constitution. Some legal scholars maintain that our legal system already contains the resources to protect individuals against unwarranted government intrusions of various kinds and that there is no need to create a distinct right of privacy. Three definitions of the right to privacy are commonly offered:

The right to be left alone. This derives from both the Warren and Brandeis definition and the decision in *Griswold*. Warren and Brandeis were concerned mainly with the publication of idle gossip in sensational newspapers. In the *Griswold* decision, Justice Brennan claimed that the right to privacy prohibits government intrusion into such fundamental decisions as whether or not to beget a child. Criticisms of this definition are three-fold. First, the right "to be left alone" is overly broad. Whereas individuals have a right to be left alone in most matters of religion and politics, the public has a right to know about some matters, such as campaign contributions. Second, some violations of privacy occur in situations where there is no right to be left alone, such as the workplace. Third, the Warren and Brandeis definition confuses privacy with liberty. A loss of liberty is neither a necessary nor a sufficient condition for a loss of privacy.

The right to have control over personal information. Privacy can also be defined as control over information about ourselves. Critics charge that this definition is too broad, since not every loss or gain of control over information about ourselves is a loss or gain of privacy. In addition, privacy cannot be equated with control, because individuals exercise control when they voluntarily divulge intimate details about themselves and thereby relinquish their privacy.

A right not to have undocumented personal information known by others. W.A. Parent defines privacy as a state in which certain undocumented (non-public) facts about a person remain unknown by others. The facts must relate to information that a majority of individuals in a given society do not want widely known. The text contends that this is the most satisfactory definition of privacy.

The Value of Privacy

The mere fact that we desire privacy does not automatically mean that we are entitled to it. Philosophers and legal theorists have used both utilitarian and Kantian arguments to show the value of privacy and to defend it as a right.

Utilitarian arguments. Some utilitarians claim that harm is done to individuals when inaccurate or incomplete information about them is used by an employer in personnel decisions. The problem with this argument is that it assumes that the consequences of invading privacy produce more harm than good. In addition, some invasions of privacy, such as surreptitious surveillance, are objectionable regardless of the consequences. Other utilitarian arguments do not regard the harmful consequences as due solely to the misuse of information; rather, a certain amount of privacy is held to be necessary for the enjoyment of some activities. Invasions of privacy change the character of our experiences and, as a result, deprive us of the opportunity to gain pleasure from them. Yet another utilitarian argument is that privacy promotes a healthy sense of individuality and freedom among members of society and a lack of privacy can result in mental and emotional stress.

Kantian arguments. Kantian arguments revolve around the concepts of autonomy and respect for persons. Surreptitious surveillance, for example, may do no harm to a person but still diminishes a person's dignity and shows disrespect for that person. The victim loses control over how he or she appears to others, and if people form incomplete or incorrect impressions of us that we have no opportunity to correct, then we are denied the possibility of being autonomous. Critics object that not all instances where a person is unknowingly watched result in deprivation of that person's free choice. Moreover, intimate relations such as friendship and love do not consist solely in the sharing of information but involve the sharing of one's total self, and friendship and love can exist and even flourish in the absence of an exclusive sharing of information.

A third argument. A more adequate justification, which combines utilitarian and Kantian elements, derives privacy from an understanding of the way individuals are socialized in a culture. According to this argument, a respect for privacy with respect to some matters is an essential part of the socialization process through which individuals develop a sense of personal identity and worth.

Justifying a Right of Employee Privacy

In the workplace, the main threat to employee privacy comes from the personal information that employers gather in the ordinary course of business. The issues that determine whether an employer respects the privacy of employees or violates their right of privacy are: the kind of information that is collected, the use to which the information is put, the persons inside and outside the company who have access to it, the means used to gain the information, the steps taken to ensure its accuracy and completeness, and the access that employees have to information about themselves.

The purpose for information gathering. The justification for an employer possessing any personal information depends on the purpose for which the information is gathered. Companies are generally justified in maintaining medical records on employees, for example, in order to administer benefit plans and monitor occupational health and safety. An employee's right to privacy is violated if the personal information is gathered without a sufficient justifying purpose, the information is known by persons who are not in a position related to the justifying purpose, or persons who are in such unrelated positions use the information for illegitimate purposes.

Resolving disagreements about purpose. Whether a purpose is legitimate can be determined by showing that it is necessary for the normal conduct of business. Thus, information that is necessary for complying with the law is legitimate. Another way of determining whether a purpose is legitimate is by asking what information both the employer and the employee need in order to form a valid employment contract. An employer is not able to freely contract with an employee without having some personal information, but other personal information is unnecessary for this purpose.

Disclosure to outsiders. Generally it is morally objectionable for an employer to disclose personal information to an outside party without the employee's consent. However, neither an employer nor an employee can be said to *own*—in the sense of having an exclusive and unrestricted right of access to and control of—the information in a company's files.

The means used to gather information. A company must also justify the *means* used to gather information. Examples of impermissible means include polygraph tests, some integrity tests, constant monitoring, and pretext interviews. These procedures indiscriminately collect more information than is necessary and are often demeaning or degrading.

Accuracy, completeness, and access. Inaccurate or incomplete information can result in decisions that are unfair to employees, and so steps should be taken to ensure both accuracy and completeness. One such step is to allow employees to have access to information about themselves so that they can challenge the information or protect themselves from the consequences.

CASE SUMMARIES

Case 7.1 Psychological Testing at Dayton Hudson

Applicants for employment as a store security officer at Target stores were required to complete a psychological test called Psychscreen that asked about personal matters, including religious beliefs and sexual practices. Several employees sued Dayton Hudson, the parent company, for invasion of privacy. In the court case, Dayton Hudson admitted that the questions invaded the applicant's privacy but argued that this was outweighed by the company's legitimate interests in hiring officers with psychological stability. The plaintiffs contended that the test had not been shown to be a reliable predictor of psychological stability and that it erroneously excluded applicants with the desired psychological traits.

Discussion Questions

1. Did the test invade the applicants' privacy? Note: the tests were scored anonymously, and no one knew the responses of any applicant. Does this make any difference?
2. Suppose that the test was proven to be highly accurate. Would the test still be unfair to the few applicants for whom the test was inaccurate?
3. Suppose that a test could be constructed that did not ask personal questions. Could such a test still be an invasion of privacy if it was designed to determine a person's psychological traits?
4. A store like Target has a responsibility to protect customers from psychologically impaired security officers. If the court case results in a ruling that a test like Psychscreen is legally impermissible, how can a company fulfill its responsibility to its customers?

Case Objectives

Psychological testing, like drug testing, raises a multitude of issues. First, are psychological traits legitimate factor in hiring decisions? The answer might appear to be obvious, but these traits are not easily defined or measured, and the predictive power of a test may be weak. Moreover the behavior of employees on the job is determined not only by their psychological traits but also by the work environment. For example, improper judgment by a store security officer might be due not to a lack of psychological stability but to a lack of training. Second, the tests themselves may be intrusive because of questions that probe intimate aspects of people's lives. How serious is this intrusiveness, and how heavily does it weigh when balanced against the needs of the employer? Third, the use of inaccurate tests and the misuse of tests that have some predictive value raise issues of fairness, especially when the test yield "false positives."

Case 7.2 Three Challenges to Employee Privacy

Dating at Wal-Mart

A Wal-Mart policy prohibits dating among employees if either one is married. A single man and a woman who was legally separated from her husband were fired when a supervisor, who knew they were dating, discovered that the woman was still married. The former employees claim that they were unaware of the policy at the time.

1. Is Wal-Mart's policy justified? Does the prohibition on dating have a legitimate business purpose? Is the purpose sufficient to outweigh the interference in employees' lives?
2. Could any restrictions on employee dating be justified? For example, IBM fired a woman who was dating a man who worked for a competitor. See *Rulon-Miller v. IBM*, 208 Cal. Reptr. 524 (1984).

Case Objectives

This case involves a policy that intrudes into one of the most intimate aspects of employees' private lives. In contrast to smoking policies, the benefit to business of a no-dating policy is less tangible and the nature of the intrusion more serious. The main question, therefore, is whether Wal-Mart's no-dating policy can be justified by a legitimate business purpose.

Is E-mail Private?

In two incidents involving e-mail, an employee is fired for reading other employees' mail and two others are fired by a supervisor who read their mail and objected to the contents. E-mail is like regular mail in some ways and unlike it in others, and so the privacy of e-mail communications is unsettled. In addition, employers have a legitimate interest in ensuring that the e-mail system is not being misused.

Discussion Questions

1. How does a company's e-mail system differ from (a) the company's internal mail system and (b) employee conversation in a lounge? Would opening envelopes in the mailroom or installing listening devices in a lounge be considered invasions of privacy? How is accessing an employee's e-mail different from these two practices?
2. If a company announces a policy of monitoring e-mail messages, then does it have the right to read employees' e-mail? Or is reading private electronic mail wrong with or without notification?
3. What questions should be considered in developing a company e-mail policy? How should these questions be answered?

Case Objectives

The main objective in this case is to apply the standards for privacy in familiar settings, such as regular mail, to a new setting that has been created by advancing technology. It is worth noting that many ethical problems arise when technological advances create novel situations for which previous standards are inadequate. Many companies are developing e-mail policies, and so the case can be used to study the process of policy development.

Video Surveillance

Employees at two companies, a trucking firm and a chemical laboratory, discovered hidden video cameras in toilet and locker room areas. The stated purpose of the hidden cameras was to gain evidence of drug use or illicit sexual activity. However, employees not involved in these activities as well as nonemployees were captured on tape. In both instances, legal action was undertaken on the basis of state laws that prohibit video surveillance in areas where people have a reasonable expectation of privacy.

Discussion Questions

1. Was the video surveillance justified in each instance by each employer's legitimate needs? Were less intrusive alternatives available to each employer? In particular, did the managers at the chemical laboratory use the best means to solve the problem?

2. Would video surveillance be less objectionable if employees and visitors were given advance notice?

3. Does it matter where the video cameras are placed, or whether they are hidden or not?

4. Many retail stores operate video cameras in order to monitor employee and customer theft. Are there any significant differences between this kind of surveillance and the surveillance in the case?

Case Objectives

Video surveillance, like other forms of monitoring, is a legitimate practice up to a point; the problem is to determine the precise limits of its legitimate use. These limits are determined primarily by (1) the degree of harm that is involved, (2) the intrusiveness of the monitoring, and the balance between harm and intrusiveness, and (3) the availability of less intrusive means.

Case 7.3 Ford Meter Box

Ford Meter Box adopted a policy of hiring only non-smokers, although current employees who smoke can maintain their jobs as long as they do not smoke on company premises. A part-time employee, Janice Bone, sought a full-time position that would make her a new hire. In order to get the new job, she agreed to quit smoking. A drug test administered six weeks later revealed the presence of nicotine, and, as a result, she was fired.

Discussion Questions

1. On what grounds could the no-smokers policy at Ford Meter Box be justified? Do employers have legitimate reasons for hiring only nonsmokers? Could these reasons be served by less intrusive means?

2. Do you agree with the "slippery slope" argument that if employers are allowed to hire only nonsmokers, then they may soon restrict employee drinking or eating habits and other lifestyle matters?

3. Should states enact so-called "smokers' rights" legislation that prohibits policies like that at Ford Meter Box?

4. Is a no-smokers policy really an invasion of privacy or a restriction of liberty? Does anything of significance depend on which way the problem is described?

Case Objectives

The justification of smoking policies is a controversial issue that focuses student attention on the power that employers have over employee's lives. Introduced with the ABC News/Prentice Hall Video Library segment "Is Nothing Private Anymore?" this topic is a guaranteed discussion starter. No-smokers policies are better described as restrictions on liberty than as invasions of privacy, but a discussion of the distinction is useful. A main objective in the case is to understand that any invasion of privacy or restriction on liberty must be justified by some legitimate business purpose and that this purpose cannot be satisfied by less objectionable means. If the purpose of the policy is to reduce insurance costs, for example, this could be accomplished by charging smokers higher insurance premiums. Some students will argue on grounds of property rights that the owner of a company like Ford Meter Box can express any legal preference in hiring employees. This argument can lead to a discussion of whether business firms are private or public institutions and whether the conclusion holds true for large, publicly-held corporations. This case can also be used to test the free-market argument that the market will limit the number of employers who refuse to hire smokers, because those that do will suffer from the loss of capable, smoking employees.

Case 7.4 Lotus MarketPlace: Households

In April 1990, the Lotus Development Company announced plans for Marketplace: Households, a CD-ROM product that would enable smaller businesses to generate mailing lists for direct marketing like those already available to larger businesses from credit bureaus. The database would contain the names, addresses, and purchasing characteristics of individuals in 80 million households and could generate mailing lists of individuals possessing a specified demographic profile. The announcement was greeted with protests by groups concerned with consumer privacy. Many privacy advocates contend that people have the right to control the information that they have provided for a mortgage or a credit card. Critics of Lotus were also concerned about the use of the product by unscrupulous businesses and about the possibility of inaccurate data. Lotus had attempted to address these objections. The data would be encrypted and users could only obtain mailing lists with a minimum of 5,000 names; consumers could "opt out" by requesting that their names be deleted from the database; and the product would be made available only to reputable businesses with safeguards against misuse (for example, the lists would be seeded with decoy names so that Lotus would receive copies of mailings to consumers).

Discussion Questions

1. Is the use of customized mailing lists a good or bad development? Is anyone harmed, and if so, how? How do such lists differ from mass mailings derived, for example, from telephone directories? Much of the information is collected from publicly available sources, and so how is consumer privacy threatened?

2. If customized mailing lists are already available to larger businesses from companies such as Equifax, is there anything wrong with providing the same service to smaller businesses? That is, is there a difference between data in a giant mainframe computer and data on a set of CD-ROMs?

3. If you provide financial information in order to obtain a mortgage, does the bank have the right to use that information for some other purpose, such as making you a special offer on investments? Suppose that the bank offers a direct marketer a mailing list of affluent people. The bank does not *reveal* information on the customers' income, but the bank enables a marketer to *use* that information (which is all that the marketer wants). Does this distinction make a difference?

4. Did Lotus satisfactorily meet the (legitimate) concerns of privacy advocates? If not, what else could the company have done? If so, did the company still fail to "educate" critics and relieve their fears?

5. Alan Westin, the privacy expert who advised the company on marketing the product, observed that "the aborigines used to believe that to take a picture of a man was to steal his soul. But the bottom line with Lotus Marketplace is that you'll get a few extra pieces of mail." Is he correct? Does receiving junk mail itself constitute an invasion of privacy?

Case Objectives

This case raises issues of *consumer* privacy about what information is collected, how it is used, who has access to it, and whether the information is accurate. One critical issue is whether information that a consumer provides for one purpose (called its *primary* use) can be rightfully used for another purpose (a *secondary* use). Should guidelines be developed for "primary use" information? (Note: federal law prohibits the secondary use of information from confidential sources except when a benefit is provided to consumers. This law explains why credit card offers are always "pre-approved;" an offer of credit is a benefit, whereas an invitation to apply for credit is not.) Discussion could focus on whether Lotus should introduce the product despite the protest. However, the customers for their other products are among those most concerned about privacy, so Lotus risks alienating a key stakeholder group. In the end, Lotus dropped the product because of public protest, but a good case can be made that the company had met the concerns of privacy advocates (except for "opting out" because names would remain on all CD-ROMs previously released). Among the lessons to be learned from this case is the need to anticipate ethical concerns and to educate the public when these concerns are not well-founded.

TEACHING STRATEGIES

1. The chapter on privacy provides a good opportunity to elicit students' experiences with testing, monitoring, searches, and other privacy-invading practices. Most students have had such experiences, especially in temporary, part-time jobs, and some of their experiences are quite astounding. Probing their feelings about these experiences often leads into a discussion of the substantial issues surrounding the topic of privacy.

2. Although drug testing does not receive much attention in the text, it is perhaps the most frequently used case for discussing privacy in the workplace. "Testing Employees for Substance Abuse" in *Cases in Ethics and the Conduct of Business* focuses on a company's deliberations in developing a drug testing policy. One of many videos on drug testing is "Drug Testing of Employees," in *Drama of the Law II: Employment Issues*, from West Publishing Division.

3. Some employees who have sought assistance from Employee Assistance Plans (EAPs) for emotional and drug-related problems have found that the information that they provided in confidence has been used against them, especially in cases where employees have filed suits against employers. Thus, privacy guarantees in EAPs provide a good topic for discussion or for student papers.

KEY TERMS AND CONCEPTS

autonomy
Griswold v. *Connecticut*
liberty
polygraph tests
pretext interviews
primary and secondary use of information
privacy
the Warren-Brandeis definition of privacy

CHAPTER EIGHT

DISCRIMINATION AND AFFIRMATIVE ACTION

CHAPTER SUMMARY

Chapter 8 is primarily concerned with ethical arguments against discrimination in employment. The chapter presents the main antidiscrimination laws, including Title VII of the Civil Rights Act of 1964. Discrimination in its many forms are explained, and suggestions are offered on how to avoid discrimination in the workplace. The chapter concludes with an explanation of affirmative action and an examination of the arguments for and against it.

CHAPTER OVERVIEW

Introduction

Discrimination in business refers to the unequal treatment of many racial, ethnic, and religious groups, as well as women, in such matters as hiring, compensation, and promotion.

What is Discrimination?

The term *discrimination* refers to a wrongful act that deprives a person of some public benefit or opportunity, such as employment or education, due to that person's membership in a group toward which there is substantial prejudice. Employment discrimination involves *unequal treatment* in personnel decisions, resulting from prejudice against a particular group. This treatment directly affects the employment status and/or terms and conditions of employment for such an individual.

Title VII of the 1964 Civil Rights Act. This act specifically addresses discrimination in employment. Section 703(a) makes it unlawful for an employer to refuse to hire or discharge an individual based upon his or her compensation or terms of employment. An employer is also prohibited from limiting, segregating or classifying employees and job applicants in any way that might deprive them of employment opportunities. Title VII defines race, color, religion, sex and national origin as *protected classes*. Congress subsequently extended the list of protected classes to include the aged (*Age Discrimination in Employment Act of 1967*), the handicapped (*Rehabilitation Act of 1973* and the *Americans with Disabilities Act of 1990*), and pregnant women (*Pregnancy Discrimination Act of 1978*).

Employers can defend themselves against a charge of discrimination by arguing that race, sex or some other characteristic is relevant to the job. Section 703(e) of Title VII makes an exception for discrimination based on sex, religion, or national origin when they are *bona fide occupational qualifications (BFOQ)*, meaning that they are reasonably necessary to the normal operation of a particular business or enterprise. The courts interpret the BFOQ exception very narrowly so that "reasonably necessary" requires employers to show that the exclusion of members of a protected class is "absolutely essential" for the conduct of business and not merely useful. Race and color are never considered BFOQs, and sex is a BFOQ only under very limited circumstances.

Disparate treatment and disparate impact. *Disparate treatment* is the explicit exclusion of members of a protected class. *Disparate impact* is unequal treatment that results not from explicit exclusion but from practices that still serve to exclude members of a protected class disproportionately. Thus, a policy not to hire women firefighters is disparate treatment; a physical strength qualification that few women can meet is disparate impact. A policy that involves disparate treatment is permissible only if it passes the BFOQ test. A policy that has disparate impact, such as a physical strength qualification for firefighters, is permissible if the qualification is substantially related to successful performance of the job (the business necessity test). The *Equal Employment Opportunity Commission* and the courts often apply the 4/5ths or 80 percent rule to determine disparate impact. If the selection rate for members of a protected class is less than 80 percent of the rate for the comparison group, then disparate impact may be assumed.

Forms of Discrimination

1. *Discrimination on the basis of sex.* Sex discrimination under Title VII is defined as discrimination based on whether a person is male or female. It does not relate to sexual orientation or marital status. Homosexuals are not a protected class under Title VII, though they are protected from discrimination by some local laws. Sexual harassment is a form of sex discrimination. The Pregnancy Discrimination Act of 1978 expanded Title VII protection by amending its phrase "because of sex" to include "pregnancy, childbirth or related medical conditions."

2. *Religious discrimination.* Religious discrimination can involve disparate treatment against an employee because of his or her religious affiliation. But most religious discrimination in employment involves conflicts between the religious beliefs and practices of employees and workplace rules and routines. Employers are required only to provide *reasonable accommodations* for an employee's religious practices which would not result in *undue hardship* to his or her business or interfere with employee safety.

3. *National origin discrimination.* National origin discrimination overlaps with discrimination based on race, color, and even religion, although it is conceptually distinct since an employer might exclude Mexicans but not other Hispanics. Qualifications that have disparate impact on nationality groups, such as being a U.S. citizen or having proficiency in English, are permitted under Title VII as long as they meet the business necessity test.

4. *Age discrimination.* The Age Discrimination in Employment Act of 1967 prohibits discrimination in employment against people over forty, unless age is a BFOQ or the company has a bona fide seniority system. Highly paid corporate executives, partners, public safety employees, and judges are among those excluded from protection under the law.

5. *Discrimination against the handicapped.* The Rehabilitation Act of 1973 and the Americans with Disabilities Act of 1990 require employers to make reasonable accommodations to employ the handicapped without enduring undue hardship. Persons with disabilities are those with a physical or mental impairment that substantially limits one or more major life activity, such as caring for one's self, walking, hearing, talking or seeing. The Americans with Disabilities Act includes alcoholism and HIV infection as disabilities.

In summary, Title VII permits three defenses for discrimination: BFOQ, business necessity, and undue hardship. BFOQ is the only permissible defense to disparate treatment and does not apply to racial discrimination; business necessity applies to disparate impact for race, sex, color, and national origin; and undue hardship applies to disparate impact for religion, age, and handicap.

Ethical Arguments Against Discrimination

Utilitarian arguments, Kantian notions of human dignity and respect for persons, and various principles of justice demonstrate that discrimination is wrong.

The utilitarian argument. Discrimination is wrong because it creates an economically inefficient matching of people to jobs. Productivity suffers when employers evaluate applicants based on non-job-related characteristics such as race or sex. Discrimination in employment is also wrong on utilitarian grounds because it combines with discrimination in other areas of life (such as education and housing) to cause poverty and related social problems.

Kantian arguments. Discrimination is wrong because it deprives people of their fundamental right to be treated with dignity and respect as fully developed human beings. *Stereotypes* lead employers to treat individuals only as members of groups, denying them the dignity and respect of equal treatment.

Arguments based on justice. Discrimination is unjust according to Aristotle's principle of proportionate equality because characteristics such as race and sex are generally irrelevant to the performance of a job. According to Rawls's contract theory, discrimination is wrong because it denies individuals the important human good of opportunity for self-development.

Avoiding Discrimination

In order to avoid discrimination, employers must carefully design and implement the hiring and promotion process. In particular, a company should perform a job analysis of positions and ensure the validity of all objective tests and subjective evaluations.

Job analysis. A job analysis avoids discrimination by enabling an employer to consider only job-related characteristics in making decisions regarding hiring and promotion. Job analysis includes a *job description* (the activities or responsibilities of a position) and a *job specification* (the qualifications that are required to perform the job). In addition, recruiting and selecting applicants in a non-discriminatory manner can be facilitated through a number of efforts, including the wide distribution of information about job openings and the involvement of significant numbers of minorities and women in the hiring and promotion process.

Objective tests and subjective evaluations. *Objective tests* are tests that measure specific knowledge, skills, intelligence, and general aptitude for work. Objective tests are legally and ethically permissible if (a) they do not have a disparate impact and (b) they are *validated*, which is to say that they have been proven to be reliable predictors of successful job performance. The Supreme Court held in the Clara Watson case that *subjective evaluations,* such as personal interviews, recommendations from superiors, rating scales, and experience requirements also must not have disparate impact and be validated. Among the biases to be avoided in subjective evaluations are: the *halo effect,* when a single trait exercises an inordinate influence on the evaluator; *stereotyping,* which occurs when assumptions about members of certain groups influence an evaluator; and the *similar-to-me phenomenon,* in which evaluators favor people who possess traits similar to their own.

Affirmative Action

Affirmative action refers to hiring, training, and promotion policies that take active steps to ensure a more balanced work force. Merely ceasing to discriminate is not always adequate to remedy past injustices to protected classes. Federal, state, and local governments enact *set-aside provisions* that require a certain percentage of government funds to be "set aside" for minority-owned businesses. The Supreme Court has generally approved affirmative action programs, although it has recently imposed more stringent requirements. The courts have laid down three conditions for permissible affirmative action plans: that an affirmative action plan not create an absolute bar to the advancement of any group, that it not unnecessarily trammel anyone's rights, and that it be temporary.

The compensation argument. The compensation argument, which is derived from Aristotle's principal of corrective justice, contends that victims of discrimination are owed preferential treatment as compensation for the wrong done to them. Critics challenge this argument by noting that the individuals who receive preferential treatment are often not the same individuals who were victimized by discrimination. Defenders of affirmative action respond that discrimination effects all members of the protected class to some degree and that other forms of compensation, such as job training, may provide better assistance to the more disadvantaged. The practical difficulty of evaluating each case of discrimination leads to the practical administrative convenience of giving preference to members of groups without regard to particulars. A second objection to the compensation argument is that the burden of providing compensation often falls on individuals who did not discriminate themselves. Proponents of affirmative action respond that this burden falls to those who, even though they may not have discriminated, benefited from the discrimination and thus should return some of their unjust gains.

Equality arguments. According to these arguments, affirmative action is justified because it provides *equality of opportunity* or *equality of treatment.* The concept of equal opportunity has two distinct interpretations, namely that everyone has an equal chance of achieving some end (prospect-regarding equality) and that everyone has the same means for achieving any end (means-regarding equality). Prospect-regarding equality aims at eliminating all factors, except for chance, that affect the distribution of goods in a society. Means-regarding equality consists of a chance to compete under fair conditions. Prospect-regarding equality requires that considerable resources be provided to the disadvantaged. If some people do not succeed, it is difficult to determine whether the initial disadvantages were offset so as to provide equality of prospects. On the other hand, means-regarding equality does not require us to address inequalities that are due to past discrimination. In addition, the conditions for fair competition are highly suspect. Because of the problems with the concept of equal opportunity, some argue that affirmative action should be justified on the grounds of *equal treatment*. The concept of equal treatment is comprised of two elements: the right to an equal distribution and the right to be treated as an equal. Ronald Dworkin argues that affirmative action policies treat people equally in the second sense of treatment as an equal if they are formulated and applied with the interests of everyone considered equally.

Utilitarian arguments. Utilitarian arguments hold that affirmative action is justified as a means for addressing deeply-rooted and pressing social problems, such as racism and sexism. Preferential treatment programs serve to combat the effects of discrimination, increase employment opportunities, break down stereotypes, and heighten awareness of discrimination. In addition, affirmative action benefits corporations by increasing the pool of job applicants and improving community relations. Affirmative action programs have undesirable consequences as well. Among these are the following:

1. *The quality argument.* Critics charge that preferential treatment programs result in the hiring of less qualified persons over more qualified persons, with a resulting decline in the quality of goods and services produced which adversely affects the whole society. Supporters of affirmative action contend that the amount of quality given up is slight, because preferential treatment does not require that *unqualified* people be hired but only that among qualified applicants, preference be given to women and minorities. In addition, the evaluation of qualifications may involve some bias against certain groups.

2. *The injury caused by affirmative action.* Affirmative action programs run the risk of hurting the people it is designed to help by creating the impression that they cannot succeed on their own, thereby undermining their confidence and self-esteem. The evidence, however, is that on the whole affirmative action has significantly helped women and minorities and led to an increase in pride, self-respect, and financial well-being.

3. *The heightening of race consciousness.* A third undesirable consequence of affirmative action is that it increases rather than decreases the importance of race and gender in a society that is striving for equality. The response to this criticism is that affirmative action is a temporary remedy for eradicating past discrimination and a necessary means for realizing the ideal of an equal society.

CASE SUMMARIES

Case 8.1 Discrimination at Texaco

In 1994, six African American employees of Texaco filed suit for racial discrimination. The suit languished in court until 1996 when the *New York Times* published damaging reports of a secretly recorded conversation in which three senior Texaco executives discussed the destruction of documents and ridiculed diversity efforts at the company. In the wake of the resulting uproar, Texaco settled the suit by agreeing to pay $141 million in compensation and set aside $35 million to improve the diversity program. The employees' suit was based on both incidents of apparent discrimination and statistics that showed Texaco to lag behind other companies in the industry in hiring and promoting members of racial minorities. The discrimination occurred despite an explicit company policy and an affirmative action plan. The problem, according to critics, was the lack of oversight and implementation.

Discussion Questions

1. Did Texaco discriminate against African American employees, or were these employees simply less qualified than others? What kind of evidence could Texaco use to show that the company's practices were not discriminatory? What kind of evidence could the employees use to support their position?
2. Could discrimination exist if there were no overt racist incidents at Texaco, that is if the only evidence were statistical? Must the plaintiffs show an *intent* to discriminate?
3. Who has the burden of proof in this case? That is, should the employees be required to show that they were discriminated against, or should the company be required to justify the statistical disparities?
4. How could discrimination occur at a company with an explicit policy and an active diversity program? What steps could Texaco take to avoid a repetition of the problem? Specifically, how should Texaco spend the $35 million set aside for the diversity program?

Case Objectives

This case provides a context for a thorough introduction to discrimination law and the analysis of discrimination. The case focuses on both incidents of apparent racial discrimination and statistics that offer evidence of a pattern of discrimination. These can be used to distinguish between *disparate impact* and *disparate treatment* with regard to discrimination and to introduce questions about the burden of proof and defenses to charges of discrimination. It is important to note that discrimination law does not require an employer to hire or promote the unqualified. The central issue in the Texaco case is whether the hiring and promotion practices were properly formulated and implemented. In this regard, the lack of follow-up studies and the use of the "high-potential" list in promotion are significant. Finally, the case raises the opportunity to explore both preventive and corrective measures. That is, what should Texaco have done before the suit to prevent discrimination from occurring, and what should they do afterwards to correct the discrimination?

Case 8.2 The Alaskan Salmon Cannery

A group of nonwhite workers at a salmon cannery in Alaska have made charges of discrimination. The entire work force is transported to the cannery's remote location and housed in specially constructed barracks. The unskilled jobs on the cannery line are held mainly by Filipinos and Native Americans. The higher-paying, unskilled, non-cannery jobs are held mainly by whites. The nonwhite workers claim that the existence of two classes of unskilled workers with different pay scales is prima facie evidence of disparate impact discrimination. They also charge that various employment practices, including nepotism, a preference for rehiring previous employees, the failure to post notices of cannery openings, and an English proficiency requirement, prevent them from filling unskilled non-cannery jobs. The managers explain that the racial composition of the unskilled cannery category is roughly equal to the racial composition of the people who apply for these jobs and to the racial composition of the Pacific Northwest region where the company operates.

Discussion Questions

1. The main complaint is that unskilled non-cannery jobs are held mostly by whites. Suppose that the company can prove that the proportion of whites in those jobs is equal to the proportion of whites in the work force in the Pacific Northwest. Would that fact refute a charge of disparate impact? What is the relevant geographical area for making comparisons?

2. Some practices, such as nepotism, rehiring previous workers, and so on, *might* be responsible for any racial imbalance in the unskilled noncannery job category, but should the complaining workers be required to *prove* this?

3. If you were a member of Congress writing the law, would you include a requirement that the plaintiffs in discrimination suits prove that an employer's practices are responsible for any racial (or sexual) imbalances?

Case Objectives

This case presents the main facts and issues in a controversial court case, *Wards Cove Packing* v. *Antonio*, which prompted the 1991 Civil Rights Act. The central issue, which is expressed in Questions 2 and 3 above, concerns the evidence required for disparate impact. Is statistical evidence alone sufficient, or must plaintiffs show that an employer's practices are responsible for any imbalance? It might seem to be unfair to hold employers responsible for imbalances that result from factors beyond their control, but the difficulty of proving that an employer's practices caused any imbalance is so great that few suits could be successful. The Supreme Court ruled that Title VII places this burden of proof on plaintiffs, and after several vetoes, Congress succeeded in 1991 in amending Title VII to remove this burden. A second issue that has been raised in several court cases concerns the relevant population for determining whether an imbalance exists.

Case 8.3 The Walkout at Wilton's

Sam Hilton, the director of human resources for Wilton's Department stores, must decide what to do about the walkout out of eight of twenty drivers who refuse to enter the Wilton warehouse to load merchandise because one of the dock workers, Roy Stone, has AIDS. Wilton has an AIDS policy statement that provides information about the disease, states that reasonable accommodations will be made to employees with AIDS, and assures that confidentiality will be preserved.

Discussion Questions

1. What should Sam Hilton do? What should he tell the disgruntled workers who walked out? What should he tell Roy Stone who has AIDS?

2. Have Hilton and other Wilton managers already made some mistakes? Hint: Consider the supervisor's demand for an explanation of Stone's requests for time off, and the apparent lack of response to the reaction of Stone's co-workers.

3. Should AIDS be considered a disability under the Americans with Disabilities Act? If you were a member of Congress, would you include this provision in the legislation?

4. The union contract obligates the company to take reasonable steps to assure the health and safety of all employees. Has the company met this obligation? If you were mediating a union grievance, how would you rule?

5. Evaluate Wilton's AIDS policy. Is it well formulated? Has it been well-implemented?

Case Objectives

This case addresses current issues of great concern, namely legal protection against discrimination for people with AIDS and the formulation and implementation of corporate AIDS policies. The case also provides some relevant information about AIDS and attempts to dispel some myths surrounding it. Although the case focuses on the immediate response to a walkout, mistakes may have already been made that prevent any satisfactory resolution of the walkout. The workers' emotional reaction underlines the point that any AIDS policy must be accompanied by extensive education and counseling. A firm stand by the company from the beginning might have prevented the walkout. Some instructors might want to consider the legal aspects of the case. In particular, what constitutes "reasonable accommodation" of employees with AIDS?

TEACHING STRATEGIES

1. A table of the major pieces of legislation and landmark court decisions would be a valuable aid. Students who have taken courses in business law or human resource management should be familiar with discrimination law, but other students may benefit from a concise summary.

2. Although the law must be central to any treatment of discrimination, a course in business ethics should not merely teach the law but explore its ethical basis. The law developed from the belief that discrimination is wrong and ought to be prohibited by law. Many of the distinctions that are drawn and defenses that are permitted reflect sound ethical reasoning; and the resolution of novel cases is often guided by ethical principles. Thus, the topic of discrimination provides a good opportunity for the instructor to explain the relation of business ethics and business law.

3. A number of aids and exercises are useful in conveying the practical problems of avoiding discrimination. Provide students with statistical data on hiring that is broken down by job category, race, and gender and ask whether the data would support a charge of discrimination. One source for data in a fictional case is "The Jones Boycott" in *Cases in Ethics and the Conduct of Business*. This case also contains an explanation of the 4/5ths rule and a memorandum summarizing discrimination law. An example of a job analysis from some company can serve to emphasize their thoroughness and careful construction. As an exercise, ask students to write a job *description* of a firefighter or a police officer; determine the job *specifications*, that is the qualifications for performing the job as it is described; and ask whether any of the specifications would exclude a woman. Other possible exercises are: (1) administer some portion of a standard objective test and discuss the potential of the test for bias; (2) conduct mock interviews for a job and ask students to detect any potential for bias.

4. It is worth emphasizing that discrimination law is compatible with hiring and promoting the best people; it requires only that companies be able to show that *that* is what they are doing. However, the difficulty of justifying hiring and promotion practices and the cost of litigation, even when employers prevail, provide incentives for companies to seek a racially and sexually balanced work force. Critics of Title VII charge that the law forces companies to adopt *quotas*. Strictly speaking, quotes (which set aside certain jobs for members of a group and exclude others from consideration) are illegal, but students often use the term interchangeably with the *goal* of a balanced work force. Although this goal need not involve the use of quotas, it may still have the same effect, and so the critics' charge that Title VII forces companies to adopt quotas ought to be taken seriously in any discussion of affirmative action.

5. Many instructors find the discussion of affirmative action difficult because of the strong emotions that the topic produces. One strategy for avoiding this obstacle to discussion is to focus on the problems faced by a company with an unbalanced work force. Describe for students the situation faced by the management of Kaiser Aluminum in the *Weber* case or by the county commissioners of Santa Clara County in the *Johnson* case, or imagine a present-day corporation with no blacks or women in higher-level managerial positions. Then ask, What is the alternative to an affirmative action plan? By focusing the discussion on the solution to a problem, affirmative action can be compared with the alternatives instead of being evaluated in isolation.

6. The problem of discrimination is a multinational corporation's foreign operations can be introduced in the teaching of this chapter or the chapter on international business. For background, see Don Mayer and Anita Cava, "Ethics and the Gender Equality Dilemma for U.S. Multinationals," *Journal of Business Ethics*, 12 (1993), 701-708. A useful case for exploring the issues in this problem is "Foreign Assignment," which is reprinted in Thomas Donaldson and Al Gini, *Case Studies in Business Ethics*, 4th ed. (Upper Saddle River, NJ: Prentice Hall, 1996), 190-192.

KEY TERMS AND CONCEPTS

1991 Amendment to the Civil Rights Act
4/5ths or 80 percent rule
age discrimination
Age Discrimination in Employment Act of
    1967
Americans with Disabilities Act of 1990
bona fide occupational qualification
    (BFOQ)
business necessity
color discrimination
compensation argument
discrimination
disparate treatment
disparate impact
equal treatment / treatment as an equal
Equal Employment Opportunity
    Commission (EEOC)
equality of opportunity
experience requirements
halo-effect
handicap discrimination

heightening of race consciousness
intent to discriminate
job specification
job analysis
job description
means-regarding equality
national origin discrimination
objective tests
preferential treatment programs
pregnancy discrimination
Pregnancy Discrimination Act of 1978
prejudice
prospect-regarding equality
protected class
Public Works in Employment Act of 1977
quality argument
race discrimination
rating scales
reasonable accommodation
Rehabilitation Act of 1973
religious discrimination

reverse discrimination
segregation
set aside provisions
sex discrimination
similar-to-me phenomenon
stereotyping
subjective evaluations

terms or conditions of employment
Title VII of the 1964 Civil Rights Act
undue hardship
unequal treatment
validatation

CHAPTER NINE

WOMEN AND FAMILY ISSUES

CHAPTER SUMMARY

Chapter 9 examines the issues of sexual harassment, comparable worth, and family-friendly programs, which affect primarily women. The chapter defines the different types of sexual harassment and each one's legal status under Title VII and discusses the development of corporate sexual harassment policies. Comparable worth, which is a proposed remedy for the pay gap between men and women, is explained, along with an examination of the main objections to it, the dispute over the causes of the pay gap, the difficulty of measuring job content, the impact of comparable worth on the labor market, and the cost of implementing comparable worth. Chapter 9 concludes by analyzing the problems of balancing work and family life, including the issues surrounding the Family and Medical leave Act and family-friendly programs that address these problems.

CHAPTER OVERVIEW

Introduction

Although women hold 46 percent of all U.S. jobs, they are concentrated in traditionally female job categories. They receive only 71 cents for every dollar earned by men (the *pay gap*). They hold only a quarter of all management positions and constitute a very small percentage of high-level executives and board directors (the *glass ceiling*). More so than men, women experience the additional challenges of sexual harassment and balancing full-time work with family obligations (called the "second shift"). Some companies have responded with family-friendly programs that provide maternity leave, flexible work hours, child care, and other benefits.

Sexual Harassment

Sexual harassment in the workplace is considered to be a form of discrimination and an illegal employment practice under Title VII of the Civil Rights Act.

What is sexual harassment? The EEOC defines sexual harassment as "Unwelcome sexual advances, requests for sexual favors, and other verbal or physical conduct of a sexual nature...when (1) submission to such conduct is made either explicitly or implicitly a term or condition of an individual's employment, (2) submission to or rejection of such conduct by an individual is used as the basis for employment decisions affecting such individual, or (3) such conduct has the purpose or effect of unreasonably interfering with an individual's work performance or creating an intimidating, hostile, or offensive working environment." Under this definition, sexual harassment falls into two categories: *quid pro quo* and *hostile working environment*. Quid pro quo harassment occurs when a superior uses his or her power to grant or deny benefits to exact sexual favors from a subordinate. A hostile working environment results when the sexual conduct of coworkers or superiors causes an employee to feel so uncomfortable that it interferes with his or her ability to work.

Sexual harassment is mainly an issue of power. Accordingly, a supervisor's harassing behavior is seen as more serious than that of a coworker. Women are more likely than men to label sexual behavior as sexual harassment. The *stereotyping* of women as sexual objects that occurs outside the workplace often leads to *sex role spillover* in the workplace and to *selective interpretation*, which inhibits efforts to remedy or prevent harassment. *Priming elements*, such as pornographic calendars, also provide a stimulus for harassment and stereotyping.

Sexual harassment as a form of discrimination. Although a number of federal laws prohibit discrimination against women, none of them explicitly addresses sexual harassment. Among these laws are: the Equal Pay Act of 1963, which prohibits an employer from offering different wages to men and women who perform substantially similar work, Title VII of the Civil Rights Act, which prohibits discrimination based on the fact that a person is male or female (unless sex is a BFOQ), and the Pregnancy Discrimination Act of 1978, which amends the phrase in Title VII "because of sex" to include any adverse employment decisions based on "pregnancy, childbirth, or related medical conditions."

A question for the courts was whether sexual harassment is a form of sex discrimination under existing laws. The Supreme Court held in *Meritor Savings Bank v. Vinson* (1986) that both quid pro quo and hostile working environment harassment constitute sexual discrimination as defined by Title VII. Quid pro quo harassment violates Title VII by treating men and women differently with regard to their terms or conditions of employment. Hostile working environment harassment also constitutes sex discrimination because it treats women differently by requiring them to endure a form of stress that can interfere with their ability to work and erode their sense of well-being. Hostile working environment harassment is more prevalent than quid pro quo but more difficult to prove. The standard used by the courts is whether a *reasonable person* would find the conduct or environment offensive. The courts have also held that the employer has a responsibility to ensure that the workplace is free from sexual harassment and that the employer is liable for harassment committed by employees and outsiders, such as customers and clients.

Preventing sexual harassment. In addition to a legal obligation to protect employees from sexual harassment, sexual harassment results in hidden costs in the form of absenteeism, low morale, decreased productivity, increased training, and employee turnover, as well as litigation and settlement expenses. Programs implemented by corporations to prevent sexual harassment and avoid these costs contain the following four elements.

1. *A sexual harassment policy.* The policy statement should come from a high level in the organization, list the kinds of conduct that constitute sexual harassment, and indicate that they will not be tolerated.
2. *Communication of the policy.* The company should effectively communicate the policy to all members of the organization through initial training and continuing education.
3. *Procedures for reporting violations.* The policy should include well-publicized procedures (both formal and informal) for handling incidents. It should also illustrate how to file and investigate complaints, provide assurances of non-retaliation, and guarantee confidentiality.

4. *The taking of appropriate action.* The policy should provide for disciplinary action in order to deter future offenses and may also provide for compensation to the victim.

Comparable Worth

Many studies show that female dominated jobs receive less compensation than comparable jobs held by males. The concept of *comparable worth* is proposed as a means for attacking this form of discrimination.

The principle of comparable worth. The principle of comparable worth holds that dissimilar jobs can be compared with respect to certain features and jobs that are similar with respect to these features ought to be paid the same. For example, if the job of secretary and painter require the same degree of skill and effort, then both jobs deserve the same pay rate. Advocates of comparable worth believe that compensation ought to be based on *job content*, which is determined by means of a *job evaluation.* Most job evaluations consider features such as skill, effort, responsibility, and working conditions in arriving at a total number of points for a job's ranking. Compensation is based on these rankings so that jobs with the same number of points receive the same pay. Private sector employers already use a similar job evaluation process to set wages for many jobs in their organizations, and employers in the public sector also use job evaluations in order to keep parity with wages in the private sector.

Two versions of the principle of comparable worth have been proposed. One version of the principle is that a job's value ought to be determined by evaluating the work performed as opposed to the value set by the market. The only morally relevant factor in setting wages is the content of the work, and all other factors, such as supply and demand, are morally irrelevant. The second version holds that workers ought to be paid the market value of the labor, but work traditionally performed by women is paid less because of discrimination. Setting wages on the basis of job content, therefore, serves to correct for discrimination in the market. The second version is much easier to justify and is the one generally advocated.

Are wage differences due to discrimination? The cause of the earnings difference between men and women is an important issue because the second version of the principle assumes that the difference ought to be corrected because it is due to discrimination. Some statistical evidence indicates that the differences in earnings is not due to discrimination but to purely economic factors. Men earn more *income* than women in part because they work more hours. Women who often voluntarily leave the work force to raise a family have shorter work histories than men and thus do not receive the earnings increases associated with experience. Men appear to invest more in *human capital* and thereby increase their productivity. The most significant factor for explaining women's lower wages is their choice of traditionally female occupations that are already undervalued by the market. Whether this constitutes discrimination depends on whether these are the only jobs available to women or whether women freely choose them. And if discrimination does confine women to female dominated jobs, then *realignment*—the entry of women into male dominated lines of work— is perhaps a better alternative than comparable worth.

Measuring job content. A second issue surrounding comparable worth concerns the possibility of measuring job content and making reliable and meaningful comparisons among jobs. Comparable worth studies themselves have a potential for discrimination. Supporters of comparable worth point out that there are factors inherent in all jobs that allow for comparison, and reliable techniques exist for measuring these factors.

The effect on the labor market. Comparable worth, according to its critics, would undermine the ability of the market to price and allocate labor in an efficient manner. This objection assumes that the current market is efficient, which it is not if employers' wage-setting practices are arbitrary and discriminatory, as advocates of comparable worth claim. In addition, some economists (called *institutionalists*) stress the importance of *internal labor markets* and *dual labor markets*, in which factors other than supply and demand play a large role.

The issue of cost. The fourth and final issue surrounding comparable worth is the cost of implementing such a system. Estimates of the cost of eliminating wage discrimination nationwide range between two billion and 150 billion dollars. Comparable worth could also have some unintended consequences, such as an increase in unemployment rates for women. Studies of Australia, which is the only country to adopt comparable worth, show that the cost and the unintended consequences are less than predicted. Supporters of comparable worth argue that if increased pay is owed to women as a matter of right, then justice requires that society bear the cost, however high.

Family and Work

The increasing prevalence of single parents and two-earner couples with children has affected the business world. The cost to employers of ignoring family burdens includes lost productivity due to stress, the loss of training dollars when workers leave, and a failure to attract the best talent. The Family and Medical Leave Act of 1993 requires companies with fifty or more employees to allow workers up to twelve weeks of unpaid leave for the birth or adoption of a child or the serious illness or injury of a family member and to guarantee the same or equivalent job and medical benefits upon return. This legislation combines with other voluntary programs developed by businesses to create a more family-friendly environment that enables employees to balance family and work life.

The problems facing employees. At least three factors impede the advancement of women in the workplace: (1) the biological function of motherhood, (2) the traditional responsibility of running a household, and (3) the stereotypes about why women work and what they want in a job. The role of mother and homemaker requires sacrifices, such as interruptions in work history, that limit women's career advancement and earning potential. Women traditionally bear most of the costs of balancing family and work life, but employers need to assume some of this cost in order to retain women in management positions. Felice Schwartz, in her article "Management Women and the New Facts of Life," declares that the cost of employing women in management positions is greater than the cost of employing men. She concludes that some of the costs related to employing women arise from corporate practices that serve little useful purpose and can easily be altered. Much of the cost involved in employing women in management positions is offset by the value that they bring to an employer. Family-friendly programs may also help alleviate poverty, crime, and other social ills.

Evaluating family-friendly programs. There are three general groups of family-friendly programs.

1. Resource and assistance programs, such as child care, guidance for care of the elderly, and counseling for family problems.
2. Programs for emergencies and occasional needs, such as extra-long leaves and financial aid for family emergencies.
3. Programs involving flexible work arrangements such as flex-time, temporary part-time status, telecommuting, and job-sharing.

The Families and Work Institute publishes *The Corporate Reference Guide*, a benchmarking guide for companies with family-friendly programs. It classifies companies as Stage I, a company with several family-friendly policies but no comprehensive program; Stage II, a company that has developed its policies into a coordinated program; and Stage III, a company that has begun to change its corporate culture. Few companies are at Stage III, and most have not yet reached Stage I.

The problems facing employers attempting to be family-friendly are many. They include the difficulty of allowing a key member of a project to take an extended leave, the unsuitability of flexible working arrangements for jobs requiring an employee's presence, some clients' resistance to job sharing, the possibility for abuse of family-friendly policies, resentment by single employees, and a lack of clarity in the Family and Medical Leave Act. The dangers to employees participating in family-friendly programs include the risks of alienating superiors, of appearing uncommitted, and of being relegated to the "mommy track." These dangers suggest that family-friendly programs are less favorable than programs which concentrate on training and succession planning for boosting women into top management.

CASE SUMMARIES

Case 9.1 Jacksonville Shipyards

Lois Robinson worked as a welder for Jacksonville Shipyards. Although she was never solicited for sex or offered favors for sex, her coworkers ridiculed her and handed her pornographic materials. The workplace was also plastered with pornographic materials, and she observed that the sexually suggestive comments increased when her male coworkers noticed that she had seen it. She was often warned to leave so that the men could exchange jokes out of her hearing. Robinson's complaints to management went unheeded, except that a "Men Only" sign appeared on the door of a trailer where she picked up her daily instructions. As a federal contractor, Jacksonville Shipyards was required to have an affirmative action plan and an antidiscrimination policy, although the shipyard's supervisors were not trained to act on the policy. Robinson subsequently filed a suit for sexual harassment against Jacksonville Shipyards.

Discussion Questions

1. Although the behavior of Robinson's male coworkers is morally objectionable, should management attempt to prevent it? Do you accept the claim that the workers have a right to post pictures in the workplace? Is this a personal problem that workers should handle among themselves?

2. Title VII does not mention sexual harassment but merely prohibits sex discrimination. Was the treatment of Lois Robinson a form of sex discrimination? Suppose that the managers of Jacksonville Shipyards admit that her treatment was morally wrong but deny that they or her male coworkers did anything illegal. Would you agree?

3. How was Lois Robinson *harmed*? No one pressured her for sexual favors; she was not denied any advancement or wage increases because of her treatment; and she did not suffer a mental breakdown. Rather, she was *offended*. Does any employee have a right not to be offended?

4. The sign "Men Only" on the trailer door might have been intended to keep Robinson from seeing pornographic material and to preserve an all-male enclave in the workplace. Is the posting of the sign morally (and legally) objectionable? Hint: what was the trailer used for?

Case Objectives

Robinson v. Jacksonville Shipyards is the landmark case that established hostile working environment harassment as a form of sex discrimination under Title VII. Thus, the case provides an opportunity to define the concept of a hostile working environment, to distinguish this kind of harassment from quid pro quo sexual harassment, and to examine the arguments for holding hostile working environment harassment to be a violation of Title VII. The case also serves to examine the role of management in preventing a hostile working environment and responding to complaints of sexual harassment. In particular, discussion can focus on the attitudes and stereotypes that contributed to the managers' response.

Case 9.2 Sexual Harassment or Business as Usual?

Selling Playboy at Dairy Mart

Dolores Stanley, the manager of a Dairy Mart, decided to remove all adult magazines, such as *Playboy* and *Penthouse*, from the store. Her superiors insisted that she put the magazines back on display because Dairy Mart should not attempt to censor its customers' reading materials. Stanley claimed that the magazines, which were in opaque plastic wrappers, were offensive to her and degrading to all women and that forcing her to sell them constituted sexual harassment.

The Swedish Bikini Team

The Stroh Brewery Company used the scantily-clad Swedish Bikini Team to promote one of its beers. Five women who worked for the brewery alleged that the company's advertising encouraged harassment by male coworkers. The company admitted that the women had been harassed by male coworkers but denied that the advertising contributed to the men's behavior, and the company pointed to its own sexual harassment policy as evidence that such conduct is not condoned.

Discussion Questions

1. Was Dolores Stanley a victim of sexual harassment? How does this case differ from one in which coworkers or customers bring *Playboy* and *Penthouse* into a workplace? Would Stanley be harassed if the magazines were on display without the opaque plastic covers?

2. Could a company's advertising *ever* contribute to an environment in which harassing behavior is more likely to occur? That is, should a company consider the impact of an advertising theme on the behavior of their own employees? In your opinion, did the Swedish Bikini Team advertising campaign contribute to the harassing behavior of the women's male coworkers?

Case Objectives

These two cases explore the responsibility of companies that choose, for commercial reasons, to utilize sexually explicit materials. Dairy Mart has chosen to sell *Playboy* and similar magazines, and the Stroh Brewery has chosen to use sexual themes in its advertising. The Dairy Mart case poses a relatively simple question: is a Dairy Mart store a hostile working environment? Even though students are apt to dismiss Stanley's complaint, it is worth comparing her situation with that of Lois Robinson at the Jacksonville Shipyards. First, the environment of the shipyard is clearly offensive by the reasonable person standard, but would a reasonable person find the Dairy Mart environment offensive? Second, the presence of offensive materials is irrelevant to the business of shipbuilding; but selling magazines is part of Dairy Mart's business, and Stanley knew or should have known that Dairy Mart stores stock the magazines. The Stroh Brewery case is more subtle. That the women were harassed is not in question, but did the company's advertising campaign make harassing behavior more likely? If so, then the responsibility of management for preventing harassment extends beyond obvious steps to such matters as the design of an advertising campaign.

Case 9.3 The Mommy Track

CEO Robert Begley wrote a memorandum to the Vice President of Human Resources, Maria Mendoza, asking her opinion about the problems with the company's family-friendly program and his ideas to address them. The turnover rate for women managers is more than twice that of men, and a disproportionate number of the women who succeed have no children. Begley proposes that these problems be addressed by creating two tracks for women, a "fast track" and a so-called "mommy track," as recommended in a *Harvard Business Review* article by Felice Schwartz.

Discussion Questions

1. Are the facts cited by Begley really problems that need to be addressed? Should these problems be addressed merely because they increase costs for the company or should they be addressed as ethical concerns?
2. Is the company's family-friendly program part of the problem? If so, should the program be eliminated or accompanied by other changes?
3. Should the company adopt Begley's proposal for a "two track" system for women employees? Does this system adequately meet the "realities" of what it takes for women to advance? Does it perhaps accept these realities too readily when more fundamental change is needed?

Case Objectives

The case introduces the impact of women's family responsibilities and of family-friendly programs on the advancement of women in corporations. The focus of the case is a controversial proposal by women's advocate Felice Schwartz for a two-track approach, which is discussed in the text. A key issue in the controversy is whether such an approach is a realistic solution to a problem that is due to forces that are largely beyond corporate control or whether it accepts these forces too readily and serves to reinforce rather than to change them. For more background, the instructor is referred to the replies to Schwartz's article in the *Harvard Business Review* and the response to the article that is cited in a footnote in the text.

Case 9.4 Is Family Friendly Always Fair?

Bill Stevens, a district sales manager, complained to Martha Franklin, the regional sales director, that the company's family-friendly program imposes undue hardship on single employees. Although he applauds the aim of the family-friendly program, Stevens cites many instances in which single employees and employees without children have covered for other employees and even been asked to accept transfers so that the company can be family-friendly.

Discussion Questions

1. Are Bill's complaints valid? Do family-friendly programs discriminate against single or childless workers?
2. Can family-friendly programs be developed that do not shift burdens to other employees? If not, should employees who bear the burden be compensated in some way?

Case Objectives

Poorly designed and implemented family-friendly programs are apt to create resentment and charges of discrimination. Such programs involve a cost, and the company avoids that cost when the burden is merely shifted to other employees. The case illustrates this danger and creates an opportunity to explore alternatives. A company can bear the cost when it provides offsetting benefits for single and childless employees. Alternatively, the case can be used to challenge family-friendly programs by asking whether corporations are obligated to accommodate employees' family responsibilities. Even if corporations have no obligation to accommodate family responsibilities, they may be forced to do so as a matter of practical necessity, in which case the problem of designing and implementing family-friendly programs remains.

TEACHING STRATEGIES

1. Sex discrimination and sexual harassment are topics of great interest, especially among female students, but instructors must be clear about their aims and careful in the means used. **Instructors are advised not to employ any simulations or role-playing games as these can lead to misunderstanding and actual harassment.** Such techniques are best left to skilled corporate trainers, who are authorized by an employer to conduct this kind of training. Some lawsuits have resulted from training sessions that have gone awry. Moreover, corporate trainers aim to modify employee behavior, whereas instructors generally focus on an understanding of the issues, for which cases are more appropriate. The main issues for classroom discussion are: (1) identifying sexual harassment, especially in borderline cases; and (2) determining managerial responsibility for preventing harassment and responding to complaints. This includes the formulation and implementation of corporate policies on sexual harassment.

2. Many videos and written cases on sexual harassment are readily available. "Sexual Harassment in the Workplace" is an eight and a half minute Nightline report in the ABC News / Prentice Hall Video Library. A 28-minute video, "The Power Pinch," is a corporate training film that provides a graphic introduction to the problem of harassment for both employers and employees. "Sexual Politics at Work" is a one-hour roundtable discussion of a fictional case; the video is one segment of the PBS series "On the Issues." "Ethics in Management," produced by Arthur Andersen & Co., contains a video vignette of a possible case of harassment. Among the many written cases, "Propmore Corporation," in *Cases in Ethics and the Conduct of Business*, is especially recommended. This case focuses on the response of a manager to a charge of harassment by a woman against a supplier representative. Sexual harassment can be a "Roshomon" situation in which each party views the conduct differently. For a case told from three points of view, see "Confronting Harassment," in Thomas Donaldson and Patricia H. Werhane, eds., *Ethical Issues in Business*, 5th ed. (Prentice Hall 1996).

3. Comparable worth is a very complex topic that combines ethics and economics. Whether discrimination is responsible for the pay gap between men and women is largely an economic question that cannot be settled by classroom discussion. A useful strategy, therefore, is to proceed hypothetically by asking whether comparable worth would be an effective remedy if the gap is due to discrimination. A discussion of this question is likely to involve a comparison of comparable worth with other means, such as realignment. The pay gap, adjusted for education and work experience, has been narrowing in recent years, and so perhaps no action is needed. A good question is, Can we wait, and if so, for how long? In addition, the distinction between the two principles of comparable worth can be used to discuss how wages ought to be set and thus ties in with Case 4.3 "Executive Compensation." A useful case on comparable worth is "The Kidd Company" in *Cases in Ethics and the Conduct of Business*.

4. Balancing family and work life is a pressing practical issue for parents and their employers, but is it really an *ethical* issue? Asking this question can lead to a discussion of the demands that employers can rightfully place on employees and the responsibility of employers for employees' private lives. The main ethical questions are, first, whether employers have an obligation to accommodate employees' family responsibilities, and, second, whether family-friendly programs themselves raise ethical concerns. Arguably, corporations are accommodating employees less from an ethical obligation and more from necessity. The more important ethical issues may arise, therefore, from the formulation and implementation of the programs themselves. Aside from fairness to single and childless employees (which is the focus of Case 9.4 "Is Family Friendly Always Fair?"), students might be asked whether fairness could be an issue in the allocation of the benefits of family-friendly policies. Some employees complain that decisions about who get the benefits are made in an arbitrary or discriminatory manner.

5. Discussions of a two-track approach (the subject of Case 9.3 "The Mommy Track") can be preceded by a nine-minute Nightline report "The Mommy Track," in the ABC News / Prentice Hall Video Library. The series also contains another Nightline report, "The Joys and Risks of the Daddy Track."

KEY TERMS AND CONCEPTS

comparable worth
Equal Pay Act of 1963
Family and Medical Leave Act of 1993
family-friendly programs
flexible scheduling
glass ceiling
hostile working environment harassment
job sharing
Meritor Savings Bank v. Vinson
pay gap
policy capturing
Pregnancy Discrimination Act of 1978
priming elements
quid pro quo harassment
realignment
reasonable person standard
reasonable woman standard
second shift
selective interpretation
sex role spillover
sexual harassment
sexual harassment policy
stereotyping
telecommuting
Title VII of the Civil Rights Act of 1964

CHAPTER TEN

UNJUST DISMISSAL

CHAPTER SUMMARY

Chapter 10 examines the justification of the employment at will doctrine in order to determine the rights of both employers and employees with regard to employee dismissal. Three arguments commonly used to justify employment at will, namely that the doctrine follows from: (1) the property rights of the owners of a business; (2) freedom of contract; and (3) the need for efficiency in the operation of a business. All three arguments are subject to limitations, however, that restrict the rights of employers and provide some protection for employees against unjust dismissal.

CHAPTER OVERVIEW

Introduction

Employment at will is a common-law doctrine according to which, in the absence of a contract, employment is an at-will relation, so that employees can leave at any time and, more importantly, employers can dismiss an employee for any reason, good or bad, or for no reason at all. A landmark case that recognized employment as a at-will relation is *Lochner v. New York* (1897), in which the Supreme Court struck down a New York statute limiting the work of bakers to sixty hours per week on the grounds that the law violated the right of both parties to contract on mutually agreeable terms. The *Lochner* decision became the basis for a series of decisions that limited worker protection and minimum wage laws, but in 1937 the Supreme Court set aside the precedent of *Lochner* and, in *West Coast Hotel v. Parrish*, upheld the constitutionality of a law setting a minimum wage for women and children. In recent years, however, the courts have allowed three kinds of exceptions to employment at will based on (1) public policy, (2) implied contract, and (3) bad faith and malice.

Property Rights and Employment at Will

The property rights argument supports employment at will by assuming that employers and employees possess some kind of property and that both parties are free to exercise the rights of property ownership in the employment relation. The historical source of the property rights argument is Locke's claim that persons have a natural right to property and a property right in their own labor. Locke's argument for property is based on the role that property, including labor, plays in satisfying human needs. However, the property rights argument is limited by three considerations.

1. Property rights are not absolute, and they must be restricted when they conflict with other rights and important societal interests. Thus, in *West Coast Hotel v. Parrish*, the importance of wholesome working conditions and freedom from oppression were held to override the property rights of the owners of a business.

2. Locke justified property rights for their role in securing human welfare and freedom, but some argue that employment at will has actually worked to impoverish a substantial portion of society and to subjugate them to the will of others. The failure of Locke's argument is due to two factors. One factor is that Locke used the term *property* in a broad sense, but the sense has been narrowed in modern society to material things; and the second factor is that the exercise of property rights has resulted in an increasing unequal distribution of property.

3. Although Locke recognized that property gives people power against the sovereignty of the state, he failed to recognize that it also gives individuals power against each other. Morris Cohen, in the classic essay "Property and Sovereignty" argues that the owners of revenue-producing property have power over others that has historically constituted political sovereignty.

Property rights in a job. Some argue that employees possess property not only of their own labor, but also in the job that they hold. If so, then property rights can be used as an argument *against* employment at will. In the case *Perry v. Sindermann*, Robert Sindermann, who was fired from his teaching job at a state university without a hearing, claimed that his job constituted property which by the Fourteenth Amendment, could not be taken from him without due process. In ruling that Sindermann was entitled to a hearing, Supreme Court held for the first time that a job is a form of property for the purposes of the Fourteenth Amendment. Justice Potter Stewart argued in *Perry v. Sindermann* that property does not consist merely in the ownership of material things but denotes a broad range of interests that are secured by "existing rules or understandings." The ruling in this case applies only to jobs in the public sector and not to private employment.

The Freedom of Contract Argument

Employment can also be viewed as a contractual arrangement between employers and employees, which arise from either an *explicit contract* or an *implicit contract* in which conditions of employment are tacitly understood and accepted by both parties. Court decisions in such cases as *Adair v. United States* (1907) have held that the right of a person to sell his or her labor is the same as the right of the employer to impose condition of employment.

The philosophical basis for freedom of contract. In both the British and American legal traditions, the basis for the freedom of contract argument derives from Locke's claim that the exercise of property rights is part of a more general freedom of action. On the Continent, the basis for freedom of contract derives from Kant's claim that autonomy involves the capacity and opportunity to make meaningful choices about matters important to us, which includes the making of mutually binding, voluntary agreements. The freedom of contract argument for employment at will is problematic because of the immense difference in bargaining power between employer and employee, and the courts have held freedom of contract cannot be justified when it prevents employees from protecting their most vital interests. There are also a number of moral and legal limits on the right of individuals to enter into contracts. Children, the mentally incompetent, those under duress, and in some cases the inexperienced and ignorant cannot voluntarily contract.

An autonomy argument. Autonomy can also be used to argue *against* the doctrine of employment at will. If people are to be autonomous, they must have not only the capacity for autonomous action but also an acceptable range of alternatives from which to choose, and some people have more alternatives from which to choose than others. In addition, bargaining between an employer and an employee takes places in a larger socio-economic setting that influences the relative bargaining strength of the two parties. Safeguarding autonomy, therefore, may consist not in leaving people free to contract without regard for their choices and bargaining power but by expanding their alternatives and by equalizing their bargaining power as much as possible.

Efficiency and Employment at Will

A utilitarian justification of employment at will is that the doctrine serves to increase economic *efficiency*. Efficiency is maximized if employers are accorded considerable leeway in determining the number of workers needed, selecting the best workers available, assigning them to the job for which they are best suited, and disciplining and dismissing workers who perform inadequately. Legal restrictions on the ability of employers to make such decisions would put legislatures and courts in the position of making business decisions. The main drawback of the argument is that the benefits accrue primarily to employers, and these benefits must be weighed against any harm to employees individually and to society as a whole. Accordingly, the courts have made three kinds of exceptions to employment at will.

1. *Public policy exceptions.* The courts have ruled that employers should not be permitted to dismiss employees when doing so in contrary to some important matter of public policy, such as protecting public health or upholding the law. Thus, employees should not be fired for refusing to commit illegal acts or for seeking benefits to which they are legally entitled.
2. *An implied contract to continued employment.* Sometimes prospective employees are given assurances in job interviews or employee manuals regarding specific grounds and procedures for dismissal. In some cases courts have ruled that these create a commitment on the part of the employer and thus constitute an implied contract.
3. *Bad faith and malice.* Even without an implied contract, a commonly accepted principle in business is that of acting in good faith. Accordingly, the courts have sometimes acted when employers have shown bad faith or actual malice in dismissing employees. Example include cases in which employees have been fired in order to prevent them from receiving a commission from a sale or to deprive them of a pension for which they would soon be eligible.

Protecting against Unjust Dismissal

In the United States, employees have less legal protection against unjust dismissal than anywhere else in the industrialized world. The main legal protection for American workers is provided by (a) contract law that enforces any existing employment contracts and contains a "good faith" standard, and (b) exceptions to employment at will based on public policy. Are these two forms of protection adequate or is there a need for additional legislation? Proponents of the status quo argue that not only would more legislation be unduly burdensome for employers, but employees also benefit by a more robust economy. Although American corporations have gone through reorganizations that have resulted in massive layoffs, proponents argue that the United States is now better positioned for global competition than the countries of Europe, where laws make reorganizations more difficult. Advocates of new legislation argue that dismissal without cause imposes a great cost or harm on employees and that the right to dismiss without cause is an irresponsible exercise of arbitrary power that ought to be curbed.

Suggestions for developing a law are provided by the 1991 Model Employee Termination Act. (Note: A model act is a proposal offered by some authoritative group to guide legislators in the creation of actual legislation.) The model act has three parts: (a) a *definition* of "good cause" in the principle that no employee should be dismissed without good cause; (b) a *method* for resolving disputes about wrongful discharge; and (c) a *remedy* for wrongful discharge. The proposed definition allows for two kinds of grounds: (a) the employee's performance, and (b) business conditions. Two important issues in the model act are (a) whether the waiver provision that allows employers to offer some benefits to employees who waive their rights under an employee termination act effectively thwarts the purpose of any act, and (b) whether arbitration, which is the proposed method in the Model Employee Termination Act, can be effective in a nonunionized setting.

CASE SUMMARIES

Case 10.1 The Firing of Robert Greeley

Robert Greeley was dismissed from his job at Miami Valley Maintenance Contractors because his company decided that it was too much trouble to withhold child support payments from his paycheck as ordered by a local judge. The company preferred instead to pay a $500 fine for refusing to comply with the court order. The Ohio law that enables a judge to order an employer to withhold child support payments was enacted in order to comply with a federal law that sought to address the problem of divorced fathers who fail to support their children. Although Ohio had been an employment-at-will state—the courts had refused to intervene when an employee was fired for reporting illegal dumping of toxic wastes, for example—the Ohio Supreme court ruled in this case that the actions of Greeley's employer undermined the ability of government to devise an effective solution for an important social problem.

Discussion Questions

1. The court's ruling applies only to Greeley's unusual circumstances. How far should the court extend this public policy exception? Are there good reasons for not extending it very far? (Hint: note the opinion in *Pierce v. Ortho Pharmaceutical Corporation.*)
2. Was the court consistent in refusing to intervene in the case of the employee who was fired for reporting the illegal dumping of toxic wastes? Are there any relevant differences between the two cases?
3. Should the state place a responsibility on businesses to help solve social problems, such as ensuring that divorced fathers make child support payments? If so, are there any limits on the social problems that businesses can be forced by government to address?

Case Objectives

This case provides not only an example of a public policy objective that can limit the right of employers to dismiss at will but also an opportunity to examine the scope of the public policy exception. What public policy objectives are important enough to create exceptions to the doctrine of employment at will? The Ohio State Supreme Court refused to offer any general principle for deciding other cases, and so students can be asked to formulate such a principle—or to decide whether such a principle is possible. The case also raises questions about the justification of a law that enlists the aid of businesses in collective child support payments. Is there any significant difference between the Ohio law and laws that require employers to withhold taxes?

Case 10.2 Waiving the Right to Sue

In an attempt to protect itself against lawsuits for wrongful discharge, a company offered all senior level employees a deal: if they would waive their right to sue the company in the event of termination, then the company would guarantee them an enhanced severance package. David Parker decided to sign the waiver. Seven years later, at the age of 58, David was dismissed and had difficulty finding a new job. He and five other employees believe that they have a strong case of age discrimination, but the waivers that Parker and two others signed pose a problem, unless they can argue that the company's offer was coercive or unfair.

Discussion Questions

1. Was the company's offer coercive? Any employee could refuse to sign and retain the customary severance package. Suppose that the enhanced severance package was customary and the company threatened to reduce the benefits of employees who refused to sign the waiver. Would not the outcome be the same? (See the analysis of coercion in Chapter 13.)
2. Was the company's offer unfair? Should any agreement to give up rights that employees have as a matter of law be legally enforceable? Suppose that a waiver had been signed by an African-American who is later terminated because of race, or by a woman who is dismissed for becoming pregnant. (Students can be also asked to consider whether it would be fair for an instructor to offer a substantial number of bonus points to students who agree not to protest their final grade in a course.)

Case Objectives

This case highlights the growing practice of offering benefits to employees in return for the employees' agreement not to sue the company on certain grounds. The practice serves to protect companies from troublesome litigation, but it also has the potential for coercion. Both the freedom of contract and autonomy arguments for employment at will can be examined in the context of offers of benefits for waivers. For example, would legal restrictions on such offers infringe on the freedom of contract of employees who might prefer such offer or deny employers a legitimate tool for reducing risk from litigation? Is employee autonomy increased or reduced by such offers?

Case 10.3 A "State of the Art" Termination

Bill Collins arrived at work one morning to find a memo telling him to attend a meeting at a nearby hotel. Once there, he met with three other persons from his department and a consultant from an outplacement firm who told the employees that they were being terminated because of downsizing by the company. The good news was that the employees would receive generous severance benefits and job-search support. The bad news, however, was that terminated employees were not to return to the workplace, nor were they to contact anyone still working for the company. The contents of their desks would be boxed and delivered to their homes, and they would have the opportunity to copy personal material from their computer files. Prepaid taxis were waiting to take them home. Bill Collins understood the danger to the company from employee sabotage but still felt humiliated, despite the efforts of the company to treat the terminated employees well.

Discussion Questions

1. Did the company strike the right balance between compassion for the terminated employees and the need to protect against possible harm? Was the humiliating treatment necessary for business reasons?

2. Do employees have any rights with regard to the manner in which they are terminated? Correspondingly, do employers "owe" terminated employees any kind of treatment?

Case Objective

This case is based on actual situations in which companies have marred the otherwise compassionate treatment of dismissed employees with a few humiliating touches. Some might argue that the generous financial benefits show the company's compassion and that employees like Bill Collins are being unduly sensitive. After all, business is about dollars and cents, not feelings. Others might argue that feelings are important as well, but how should feelings be weighed against the need of a company to protect against the possibility of employee sabotage?

TEACHING STRATEGIES

1. Although employment at will is deeply ingrained in American law, the doctrine is unfamiliar and suspect to many students who believe that due process and a just cause are morally, if not legally required. Therefore, instructors may need to emphasize the force of the traditional arguments for employment at will. Students should also be made aware that employees are free to bargain for protection against unjust dismissal and that many employers offer such protection in order to attract and retain desirable employees. Whether employment is at-will often depends on how much employees value guarantees of due process and dismissal only for cause and on how much bargaining power employees have.

2. The justification of employment at will on the grounds that the employment relation involves the exercise of property rights by both employers and employees is a crucial part of this chapter, and so it is important to explore the various kinds of property. Ask students, for example, about the sense in which stockholders "own" a corporation, so that they understand that stockholder ownership consists of voting rights, the right to dividends, residual claims in the event of bankruptcy, and so on. Cohen's thesis that property rights create a kind of political sovereignty is difficult for many students to understand and may require some explanation. Students might be asked to consider whether the power of insurers to determine the medical treatment that people receive constitutes a form of power like that traditionally held by government.

3. This chapter provides an opportunity to discuss the phenomena of downsizing and the changing contract between employers and employees. Many companies now explicitly deny any promise of lifetime employment and stress the need for employees to manage their own careers. The case "ABC Corporation and Employment Stabilization" in *Cases in Ethics and the Conduct of Business* raises the question of whether stable employment should be one of the aims of a business.

4. Ask the students to relate stories of parents, friends, siblings—or even themselves—regarding termination from a job. Note particularly whether or not there was any explicit or implied employment contract given to the person when he or she was hired. Note also how the termination was both reported and carried out.

5. Ask students to research the state's law on employment at will and also the policies of some prominent local corporations. In particular, does the state require or do local corporations provide either a *just cause* or a *due process* requirement in the event of termination?

KEY TERMS AND CONCEPTS

autonomy
due process
employment at will
explicit/implied contract
freedom of contract
just cause
Lochner v. *New York*
Perry v. *Sindermann*
political sovereignty
property rights
public policy exception
West Coast Hotel v. *Parrish*

CHAPTER ELEVEN

MARKETING, ADVERTISING, AND PRODUCT SAFETY

CHAPTER SUMMARY

The first section of this chapter examines two competing theories of marketing—the marketing concept and consumerism—and applies these theories to specific problems in packaging and labeling, pricing, sales techniques, and anticompetitive marketing practices. The second section examines the ethical issues surrounding the content and techniques of advertising. It addresses the morality of persuasion and behavior control, including a discussion of the dependence effect and the concept of rational persuasion in the making of consumer choices. This section also discusses the definition of deceptive advertising and the application of this definition to examples of advertising claims. The third section explores the responsibility of manufacturers for the safety of products and explains and evaluates three theories of product liability—due care, the contractual theory, and strict liability.

CHAPTER OVERVIEW

Marketing

Marketing is defined as "the performance of business activities that direct the flow of goods and services from producer to consumer or user." Within this broad definition, ethical issues occur in the functions of product development, distribution, pricing, promotion, and sales.

Consumerism and the marketing concept. The consumer movement that began in the early 1960s with several muckraking books spawned many pieces of protective legislation, including the Fair Packaging and Labeling Act (1966), the Truth-in-Lending Act (1968), the Child Protection and Toy Safety Act (1969), the Consumer Product Safety Act (1972), and the Magnuson-Moss Warranty Act (1975). This movement arose despite the fact that business had long operated on the basis of the *marketing concept*, which stresses consumer satisfaction. Traditionally, producers are understood to have several rights, which are limited only by the usual rules of fair market exchanges. These rights are:

1. To make decisions regarding the products offered for sale, such as their design and style.
2. To set the price for products and all other terms of sale, including warranties.
3. To determine how products will be made available to consumers.
4. To promote products in any way that producers choose.

The consumer movement sought to balance the rights of producers with a list of buyers' rights that include the rights to:

1. Be protected from harmful products.
2. Be provided with adequate information about products.

3. Be offered a choice among products that they truly want.
4. Have a voice in the making of marketing decisions.

Packaging and labeling. Consumers need a certain amount of information to make rational choices, but often this information can be easily obtained only from the manufacturer. But how much information is a manufacturer obligated to provide, and to what extent are consumers responsible for informing themselves? Two pieces of legislation that regulate packaging and labeling attempt to provide a fair balance between consumers' need to know and the ability of manufacturers to sell. The Fair Packaging and Labeling Act of 1966 requires that each package list the identity of the product; the name and location of the manufacturer, packer, or distributor; the net quantity; and, as appropriate, the number of servings, applications, and so on. Additionally, the Nutrition Labeling and Education Act of 1990 requires that packaged food products contain relevant nutrition information, such as fat, cholesterol, and salt content, and limits the use of health claims, such as *low fat*, *light*, and *healthy*.

Pricing. The proliferation of products at different prices, price codes that can be read only by sales personnel, the omission of essential extras, and hidden costs all serve to prevent consumers from calculating the true price of products. The problems can be alleviated by requiring uniform pricing and the disclosure of product information, including standard measures of relevant factors.

The obligation to provide information. What is the justification of consumer protection legislation? In traditional free market theory, producers are obligated only to be truthful and to fulfill any warranties. Consumers bear the primary burden for informing themselves about products. *Caveat emptor* is the rule. An alternative rule holds that manufacturers have an obligation to provide information that consumers cannot reasonably obtain for themselves. A reason for abandoning *caveat emptor* is that in a modern industrial economy it is too difficult for consumers to inform themselves adequately. Manufacturers can provide the needed information at a much lower cost.

Deceptive and manipulative marketing practices. Deception involves creating or taking advantage of false beliefs that significantly interfere with the ability of consumers to make rational choices. Some common deceptive pricing and sales practices include "suggested retail prices" for products seldom sold at that price, "cents off" and "introductory offers" that offer no bargains, bogus clearance sales, deceptive packaging and labeling, and warranties that are too complicated to be understood by the average consumer. Manipulation is the non-coercive shaping of the alternatives available to consumers or their perceptions of those alternatives which effectively result in consumers being deprived of a choice. Examples include 1) customary pricing, in which manufacturers reduce the amount of a product per unit in order to maintain the same price, 2) bait and switch, which occurs when consumers are lured into a store by a low cost, low quality item, and then switched to a higher priced product, and 3) high-pressure sales techniques. Deceptive and manipulative marketing practices are ethically objectionable because they both impair consumers' ability to make rational choices and lead them to make choices that they would not otherwise make.

Marketing research. Marketing research collects data about consumers using such techniques as in-depth surveys, field studies, and controlled laboratory experiments. Unethical marketing research practices arise when research participants are deceived about the purpose of a study, when the "research" is done only to make a sales pitch (a practice known as *sugging*), or when retailers, through the use of database marketing, are able to construct detailed profiles on individual customers' buying habits and make customized offers.

Anticompetitive Marketing Practices. The main anticompetitive marketing practices are price fixing, price discrimination, resale price maintenance, reciprocal dealing, tying arrangements, and exclusive dealing. Price fixing is an agreement among two or more companies operating in the same market to sell goods at a set price. It is usually done horizontally, among different sellers at the same level of distribution, though it can be vertical, between buyers and sellers at different levels. Sellers engage in price discrimination when they charge different prices or offer different terms of sale for identical goods sold to different buyers. Resale price maintenance is a practice whereby products are sold on the condition that they be resold at a fixed price. Reciprocal dealing is a sale in which the seller is required to buy something in return. A tying arrangement exists when one product is sold on the condition that the buyer purchase another product. And in exclusive dealing, a seller provides a product on the condition that the buyer not handle competing brands.

Most of these unethical marketing practices are also illegal as a result of antitrust statutes such as the Sherman Act (1890), the Clayton Act (1914), the Federal Trade Commission Act (1914), and the Robinson-Patman Act (1936). The main objection to most anticompetitive marketing practices is that they lead to the formation of monopolies, which drives competitors out of business and increases prices to consumers. Resale price maintenance, reciprocal dealing, tying arrangements, and exclusive dealing are also objectionable because they distort the market mechanism for setting prices. The ethical objection to all of the above-mentioned practices is generally that they are not fair forms of competition.

Advertising

Advertising is "a paid form of nonpersonal communication about an organization and/or its product that is transmitted to a target audience through a mass medium." Other types of promotional activity include publicity—press releases and other public relations efforts that do not involve the purchase of time or space from the mass media, sales promotion—contests, coupons, and free samples that are not strictly a form of communication, and personal selling, which is selling done by shop clerks and telephone solicitors that is neither impersonal nor done through the mass media. A distinction is made between *product*, *corporate*, and *advocacy* advertising. Product advertising involves the promotion of a product or a service. Corporate advertising, on the other hand, is done to enhance the image of a corporation, and advocacy advertising is used to advance an issue or a cause.

Advertising is criticized for many reasons, including its exaggerated claims, irritating repetition, objectionable products, and the creation of a culture of consumerism. Some economists argue that advertising is a wasteful and inefficient activity that stifles competition and leads to monopoly conditions. Others charge that advertising appeals to emotions by manipulating needs and creating wants that hinder consumers' ability to make rational choices. There is a great concern about advertising's potential for behavior control through the exploitation of psychological research into human motivation. Finally, the charge of the Federal Trade Commission to protect the public against deceptive advertising raises questions about the meaning of deception and the conditions for claiming that an ad is deceptive.

Persuasion and Behavior Control. Although advertising and propaganda have limited power to change people's basic attitudes, modern advertising techniques are reasonably successful in playing on natural human desires for security, acceptance, and self-esteem in order to influence consumer choices, and some economists and philosophers contend that certain types of advertising cross the boundary between legitimate and unacceptable forms of behavior control.

The economist John Kenneth Galbraith argues that in modern society wants are being created through the same process of production by which they are satisfied. This dependence effect undermines the traditional economic argument that justifies production on the grounds that it satisfies consumer demand. This argument holds that the value of goods arise from their role in satisfying the needs and wants of consumers and that consumers themselves are the best judges of what will satisfy their needs and wants (the principle of *consumer sovereignty*). However, production cannot be justified for the reason that it satisfies urgent wants if those wants are created in order to facilitate production. The dependence effect also creates an imbalance between the abundance of private consumer goods and the dearth of public services because wants are created only for those products that can be packaged for individual consumption and sold at a profit.

F. A. von Hayek, a critic of the dependence effect, observed that every want beyond the most primitive needs for food, shelter, and sex do not originate within a person but are created by outside forces and that these created wants are no less urgent or important because their source originates outside the person. Galbraith argues that some wants are less worth satisfying than others, but von Hayek points out that the distinction cannot be made in terms of the *source* of the want. However, another criterion for judging the value of our desires is *rationality,* or the suitability of a desire for achieving some end or purpose. Thus, a desire for a product that appeals to a yearning for status is an irrational desire if the product cannot provide status.

Is the influence that advertising exerts on consumers consistent with a respect for personal freedom and autonomy? Some kinds of persuasion can wrongfully deprive people of the freedom to make consumer choices. Both *subliminal communication* and *product placement* are morally objectionable for the reason that they attempt to persuade people in ways that deny them the opportunity to engage in critical evaluation and thus act on people without their knowledge or consent. The distinction between morally permissible and morally objectionable forms of persuasion might be made by distinguishing between *rational* and *nonrational persuasion.* One test of this latter distinction is whether people can be aware of what is happening to them. However, more psychological research on the effects of advertising and mass communication and a better understanding of the motivation for choices are needed in order to apply this test. Finally, whether persuasion is rational or nonrational depends, in part, on the *ends* for which techniques of persuasion are used and not merely the techniques or means.

Deceptive Advertising. Whether an ad is deceptive is not easy to determine due to the lack of a precise definition of *deception.* Deception does not depend merely on the truth or falsity of the claims made: An ad can be deceptive without containing a false claim and it can contain a false claim without being deceptive. The FTC has not offered a precise legal definition of deceptive advertising. David Gardner's definition states that deception occurs when a consumer, after viewing or hearing an ad, has impressions or beliefs that do not constitute reasonable knowledge and the impressions are false or misleading. The objections to this definition are threefold. First, an ad is not deceptive merely because it fails to ensure that a consumer has reasonable knowledge. Second, the definition does not consider who is deceived and considers any ad to be deceptive even if only the most gullible consumers were misled. Third, the definition cannot be applied to determine deception until some standard of reasonable knowledge is specified.

Carson, Wokutch, and Cox attempt to patch up Gardner's definition by holding that an ad is deceptive if it causes a significant percentage of potential consumers to have false beliefs about the product. Boatright questions this revised definition not only because the phrase *significant percentage* is unspecified but because the definition requires that the ad *cause* the false beliefs, whereas an ad could be deceptive by merely taking advantage of a false belief that consumers already hold. A more satisfactory definition is that deception occurs when a false belief, which an advertisement either creates or takes advantage of, substantially interferes with people's ability to make rational consumer choices. One shortcoming of this definition is its failure to define *rational consumer choice*; another is the meaning of *substantially interferes*. Two factors are relevant to the notion of substantial interference: (1) the ability of consumers to protect themselves and make rational choices and (2) the seriousness of the choice that consumers are making. The Campbell Soup health ads exemplify both factors. Consumers could not easily protect themselves by obtaining information on the salt content of the Campbell soups being advertised, and the decisions consumers make regarding their health are of great importance.

Theories of Product Liability

Three theories—due care, contractual, and strict liability—are commonly used to determine when a product is defective and what is owed to victims who have been harmed by defective products. Each appeals to different grounds for its ethical justification.

The Due Care Theory. According to this theory, manufacturers are obligated to take all reasonable precautions to ensure that their products are free of defects likely to cause harm. This theory finds its legal expression in tort law, according to which persons are liable for injury to others if the injury results from negligence. Negligence is defined as falling below the care that a "reasonable person" would take to protect others from injury. We are all required to exercise due care to avoid injury to others, but a manufacturer can be assumed to know more than the average person about its product and thus can be legally required to exercise a greater degree of care. The standard of due care applies to design, materials, production, quality control, packaging, and information provided to users. The courts have also maintained that due care extends to ensuring that a product is safe for all reasonable foreseeable uses, including misuse by the consumer. Manufacturers are especially liable when they encourage such misuse (which is called "invited misuse").

Generally courts have developed a flexible standard for due care that is derived from Justice Learned Hand's famous definition of *negligence* in which negligence involves the interplay of (1) the probability of harm, (2) the severity of the harm, and (3) the burden of protecting against the harm. The courts have considered whether the standards for due care should merely reflect scientific knowledge at a given time or whether they should anticipate *future* hazards of products. In some cases, the courts have rejected the so-called *state of the art defense*—in which a company contends that it exercised due care as defined by the scientific knowledge and technology of the time. As a legal doctrine, the due care theory is difficult to apply for two reasons. First, the focus of the theory is on the *conduct of the manufacturer* rather than on the *condition of the product*. Second, common law allows companies two defenses: They can maintain that an injured consumer contributed to the injury (*contributory negligence*) or assumed the risk of injury (*voluntary assumption of risk*). For these reasons the due care theory is rarely used today in product liability cases; there are easier ways for injured consumers to secure compensation.

The Contractual Theory. According to the contractual theory, the obligations of a manufacturer to a consumer are contained in an implicit or explicit sales contract. Common implicit contractual obligations include an *implied warranty of merchantability* and an *implied warranty of fitness*, according to which the seller implies that the product is of an acceptable level of quality, fit for the purpose for which it is ordinarily used, and free from dangerous defects. An *express warranty* arises from any affirmation of fact or promise made by the seller to the buyer about the product. The ethical basis for the contractual theory is *fairness* in commercial dealings. Both parties to the contract must enter into the contract freely, and have adequate information about the product in question. But even when the manufacturer is unaware of a defect, the cost of any accident ought to be borne by the manufacturer because the product was sold with the understanding that it posed no hazards except those revealed to the consumer.

First, the understandings in sales agreements are not very precise, so the theory leaves consumers with little protection except in the case of grossly defective products. Second, written contracts may sharply limit the right of an injured consumer to be compensated, especially if the product is sold with an explicit disclaimer of any warranty. Both of these are illustrated in the case of *Henningsen v. Bloomfield Motors*, in which the sales contract warranty, located in paragraphs that were difficult to read and not highlighted in any way, was specifically limited to the replacement of defective parts and did not include liability for personal injuries resulting from defective parts. The court ruled that considerations of justice overrode an otherwise valid contract. In addition to the "sharp bargain" that has been made, the consumer lacked the power to bargain for a better warranty (most manufacturers offered the same warranty) and lacked the ability to inspect the car for defects.

Strict Liability. This third theory, now gaining wider acceptance in the courts, holds that manufacturers are responsible for *all* harm resulting from a dangerously defective product, even when due care has been exercised and all contracts observed. The mere fact that a product is put into the hands of consumers in a defective and potentially dangerous condition is sufficient for holding the manufacturer liable. Strict liability does not require that a victim of an accident be in a direct contractual relation with the manufacturer—a requirement known as *privity*. Before the development of strict liability, the requirement of privity had already been weakened by the courts in two cases: *MacPherson v. Buick Motor Company* (1916), in which the New York State Court of Appeals ruled that privity was not necessary when there is negligence, and *Baxter v. Ford Motor Company* (1934), in which the court held that the wording of an advertisement can create an implied warranty even in the absence of a contractual relation. Strict liability was first accepted by a court in *Greenman v. Yuba Power Products* (1963), in which the user of a power tool suffered injury. The court ruled that the relevant consideration was not whether the company was negligent in the design and construction of the equipment, but rather whether the tool caused injury when used in the intended way.

Strict liability can be justified by appealing either to *efficiency*—securing the greatest amount of protection at the lowest cost—or *equity*— distributing the costs of injuries fairly. Both arguments recognize that certain costs are involved in preventing accidents and in dealing with the consequences of accidents that do occur. Insofar as manufacturers avoid the cost of reducing accidents, this cost is passed along to consumers, who pay for the injuries that result. So how can the total cost to both manufacturer and consumer be reduced to the lowest possible level? And how should the cost be distributed between manufacturers and consumers? On the basis of *efficiency*, manufacturers ought to bear the cost of preventing accidents insofar as they are able to protect consumers at less cost. On the basis of the *equity* argument, manufacturers again ought to be primarily responsible because they generally make profits on the sale of their products.

The primary stumbling block to strict liability is that it ignores the determination of who is at fault for an injury. Strict liability thus forces manufacturers and consumers to give up a right they have in the due care theory, namely the right not to be forced, when they are not at fault, to contribute to the compensation of accident victims. Advocates of strict liability respond that everyone benefits from its method of paying compensation, because (a) this method ensures that all victims of accidents from defective products will be compensated at the lowest overall cost, and (b) there will be fewer accidents because manufacturers will take more precautions. On the other hand, product liability covers many different types of accidents, and the most efficient or equitable system for one kind of accident may not be so for another. Second, the threat of liability suits can stifle manufacturers' innovation. For these reasons, many business leaders have pressed for uniform product liability laws and upper limits on awards to injured consumers.

CASE SUMMARIES

Case 11.1 Dow Corning's Breast Implants

Dow Corning developed the original silicone breast implant and was the leading manufacturer of the product. Little testing was done on the original breast implants because the company believed silicone to be biologically inert, and adverse test results were disregarded for a variety of reasons. In 1975, Dow Corning developed a new implant that was more pliable but also more prone to leakage. Again the company did little testing, despite questions from its own engineers about the possible consequences of silicone leaking into the body. Additionally, the company did not respond to concerns from sales personnel about the leakage. During the 1980s, as an estimated two million women received these implants, thousands began to experience severe headaches, unexplained rashes, joint and muscle pain, weight loss, and extreme fatigue. Many women and their doctors believed that silicone in the body was causing a variety of autoimmune diseases. In 1991 Dow Corning was found guilty of manufacturing a defective product and fraudulently concealing evidence of safety problems. The company was ordered to pay a $7.3 million settlement. In 1992 the FDA ruled that breast implants were not proven safe and ordered the product off the market except for limited cases of reconstructive surgery. In 1994, Dow Corning contributed $2 billion to a $4.3 billion settlement fund for women suffering from the implants. Because of continuing suits, Dow Corning filed for bankruptcy protection in May 1995. Ironically, several recent extensive studies involving large populations of women with implants have found no increase in autoimmune diseases or any other illnesses, and the prestigious *New England Journal of Medicine* questioned the need for the FDA to pull the implants from the market.

Discussion Questions

1. Even if, for the sake of argument, silicone breast implants are eventually shown to be safe, did Dow Corning fail in its responsibility to conduct the appropriate tests?

2. Who is responsible for protecting women against possibly unsafe implants? The manufacturer? The surgeons who have a responsibility to advise their patients? The government, which at the time did not regulate medical devices? The women themselves who chose to have implants?

Case Objectives

This case addresses only a few of the many complex issues that are raised by the crisis at Dow Corning. For a fuller version, see "Dow Corning and the Silicone Breast Implant Controversy" in *Cases in Ethics and the Conduct of Business*. The main issue in the shorter version in the textbook is the responsibility of a manufacturer for ensuring the safety of a product. In particular, how much testing is a manufacturer obligated to undertake before a product is placed on the market? Even if silicone is shown eventually to be harmless, it can still be argued that the breast implants are a "defective product" because of inadequate testing. That is, a product should not merely be safe but should be known to be safe. The fuller case allows students to explore the internal and external factors at Dow Corning that allowed the crisis to develop, to assess the role of physicians, lawyers, government, and society in the crisis, and to develop steps that Dow Corning managers could have taken to prevent or contain the crisis. The video "Silicone Breast Implant Safety and Dow Corning" in the ABC News / Prentice Hall Video Library provides a good "discussion starter."

Case 11.2 Volvo's "Bear Foot" Misstep

In 1990, Volvo ran ads that showed a monster truck with oversized tires riding over a row of cars. Every car was crushed but a Volvo station wagon, thereby conveying the company's advertising message of strength and safety. The catch was that the production crew for the ad had reinforced the roof of the Volvo with lumber and steel and partially sawed through the roof supports of the other cars. The company defended the rigging as an effort to conduct the demonstration safely and to allow the Volvo to withstand the repeated runs required for filming. The claim made in the ad was not false because Volvo engineers had determined that the roof could withstand the weight. Volvo and its ad agency (which subsequently resigned the $40 million Volvo account) had previously been criticized for two other ads, one that showed a large truck perched on top of a Volvo and another that stacked the cars seven high. In both ads, the bottom of the Volvo was supported by jacks placed between the tires.

Case Questions

1. Is the Volvo monster truck ad deceptive? Does the ad make any false claims or produce any false beliefs in consumers' minds? If so, do these false claims or false beliefs harm consumers in any way? Why are they objectionable?

2. Since the ads attempted to recreate the results of an actual monster truck rally in Vermont, could Volvo avoid a charge of deception by identifying the ads as a dramatization rather than as an actual demonstration?

3. Food ads often use mock-ups—replacing ice cream with mashed potatoes, for example—in order to produce more realistic images and to facilitate filming (real ice cream would melt under studio lights). Could the reinforced Volvo be considered a mock-up?

4. Do you accept the company's contention that the ads with cars and trucks atop a Volvo were intended to make a claim about the strength of the frame and not the strength of the tires and suspension system? Because the strength of the frame and not that of the tires and suspension system is critical for the safety of a car in a crash, are consumers harmed if they infer the unintended claim about the strength of the tires and the suspension system?

Case Objectives

Although the Volvo monster truck ads clearly involve deception, the company defenses have some plausibility and provide a good basis for class discussion about the meaning of deception. In particular, the case raises the issue of intentions versus results. Are the claims that the company intended, or the claims that consumers actually infer, relevant in deciding whether the ads are deceptive? The case also focuses on the question of whether consumers are actually harmed by the deception, since the false beliefs that consumers might infer would not necessarily impair their ability to make rational consumer choices.

Case 12.2 The Target Marketing of Cigarettes

Target marketing is an effective means for increasing sales by tailoring products to the needs and wants of specific consumers, but the R.J. Reynolds Tobacco Company was criticized in 1990 for its development of two new cigarette brands that were targeted at specific markets. One of the brands, named Uptown, was designed to appeal to blacks, and the other, named Dakota, was intended to attract young, blue-collar white women. The introductions of both brands, however, were scuttled following protests from outraged civil rights and women's groups.

Discussion Questions

1. What is wrong with marketing to specific groups? If marketing cigarettes to any group (such as adult smokers) is permissible, what is wrong with targeting more specific groups? Are the groups targeted for Uptown and Dakota especially vulnerable in any way? Could objections be raised to the target marketing of any other type of product to these groups? (Hint: consider the controversy over the marketing of sports shoes.)

2. The development of Uptown and Dakota was based on extensive marketing research done on the preferences of the targeted groups. If there is something unethical about developing products that target these groups, is there also something unethical about conducting the marketing research that leads to the development of these products?

3. Inner-city black neighborhoods are saturated with billboards for alcohol and tobacco products, while affluent whites generally have enough wealth and influence to banish billboards entirely from their neighborhoods. Is this just an economic (and political) fact of life, or does it constitute a kind of exploitation? (Note that affluent people can be reached by advertisers in other ways, such as through magazines that contain many ads for alcohol and tobacco products, so it is not clear that some groups are more targeted than others.)

4. After canceling the test marketing for Uptown, an executive from Reynolds remarked, "Maybe in retrospect we would have been better off not saying we were marketing to blacks. But those were the smokers we were going after, so why shouldn't we be honest about it?" Is this executive right? Could the company have avoided this public relations mishap by being less honest about its motives?

Case Objectives

The development of Uptown and Dakota is a textbook example of marketing that would be unobjectionable for almost any other product (although the marketing of sports shoes has raised similar concerns) or for any other group (consider the targeting of Absolut vodka to yuppies, for example). This case raises questions about standard marketing principles and, in particular, about the basis for the outcry against the marketing of these two products. The explanation that these products *harm* fails to distinguish the objections to the development of Uptown and Dakota from the development of any other cigarette brands. A more promising explanation is that certain vulnerable groups are being *exploited*. Target marketing is beneficial when it better satisfies the preferences of a group, but the same practice can lead to exploitation if the group is already vulnerable. This case thus raises broader questions, such as: Can marketing be exploitive? And if so, do marketers have an obligation to avoid such exploitation?

TEACHING STRATEGIES

1. The purpose of this chapter is to examine the ethical issues that arise between businesses and consumers. It is helpful to stress that the *caveat emptor* principle has been slowly eroding for several decades. Consumers now demand fair treatment, more information in order to make rational consumer choices, and a higher level of safety. Yet there are limits to the responsibility of marketers toward consumers. Much of class discussion should focus on where to draw the line and how to draw the line in a principled way.

2. Ask students to share their experiences of unfair marketing practices either as a consumer or as a salesperson. Ask students who have held sales positions to relate the instructions they were given for dealing with customers. Or ask students to find examples of questionable marketing techniques in newspaper and magazine advertising. They can look for questionable practices, such as introductory offers, bogus clearance sales, and deceptive packaging and labeling. The case "Dave Namer" in *Cases in Ethics and the Conduct of Business* consists of an interview with a professional salesperson who candidly describes the tricks of the trade. Instead of assigning the whole case, instructors may read aloud portions and ask students to evaluate the practices.

3. Ask students to present and discuss examples of advertising that they consider to be deceptive or otherwise objectionable. The examples that students offer tend to be drawn from magazine clothing advertisements that use young models in sexually suggestive poses. These ads can be used to explore questions about the impact of advertisers on sexual morality. For example, some critics charge that advertising encourages sexual activity without teaching about such problems as unwanted pregnancy and sexually transmitted diseases.

4. Students are generally skeptical that advertising is capable of strongly affecting behavior, despite the faith of marketers in advertising's effectiveness. The argument "Why would sellers pay all that money if advertising has no effect?" does little to change students' attitudes. A stronger argument is presented in a thirty-minute video of an illustrated lecture by Jean Kilbourne, "Still Killing Us Softly: Advertising's Image of Women," which is available from Cambridge Documentary Films, P.O. Box 385, Cambridge, MA, 02139, telephone 617-354-3677. The main thesis of this provocative video is that advertising affects women's images of themselves and conveys stereotypes to men that impede women's economic progress and even leads to violence against women.

5. *Cases in Ethics and the Conduct of Business* contains two cases on deceptive advertising. The case "Litton Industries, Inc." explores a FTC charge that Litton misrepresented the results of surveys and other statistical data in advertising claims that the company made for a microwave oven. "Natural Cereals" is a managerial case in which a young marketer for a ready-to-eat cereal company is called upon to design an effective yet responsible advertising campaign and to decide whether to include problematical cancer-prevention claims.

6. Students often have difficulty understanding the rationale for strict liability. An effective strategy is to focus on inherently dangerous products, such as ladders, lawnmowers, and power saws, and ask students: (1) who should bear the cost of injuries from these products, and (2) how can the cost be reduced to the lowest level? If students hold that consumers should bear the costs of their own injuries, ask: "Suppose you slipped on a rung of a ladder and the accident could have been avoided if the manufacturer had designed the rung to be more slip-resistant—and the manufacturer saved money by not using the safer design." This question enables students to see that avoiding accidents involves a cost and that without strict liability manufacturers can force consumers to bear that cost. The cost of the safer design will be passed on to consumers in the form of higher prices, but consumers are still better off because they have reduced the risk of paying for an expensive accident. In addition, the risk of accidents can be reduced more by manufacturing safer products than by encouraging safer use by consumers. As such, strict liability provides the right incentives to manufacturers. The key to this strategy is in shifting the focus of discussion from "Who's to blame?" to the social problem of how to reduce injuries from consumer products.

7. Issues in pricing and product development in the pharmaceutical industry are presented via two cases in *Cases in Ethics and the Conduct of Business*. These are *Burroughs Wellcome and the Pricing of AZT*, which concerns the controversy of the high price that Burroughs Wellcome initially charged for an AIDS drug, and "Hoechst-Roussel Pharmaceuticals, Inc.: RU 486," in which executives of a French-based company must decide whether to market a controversial drug for terminating pregnancy, a so-called "morning-after pill."

8. A 60-minute video, "Products on Trial" in the "On the Issues" series, explores a number of problems surrounding product liability, including the effect of product liability on product development, the level of acceptable risk, and the response to product liability suits. A panel of experts discusses a hypothetical case of a company that develops a male contraceptive drug that may be responsible for some birth defects.

9. Although the Ford Pinto case is rather dated, it still elicits spirited student discussion. Many print versions of the case are available, and one video version is: "Product Safety: Is Your Car Safe?," in Harvard Business School, *Ethics in Management: Video Supplement*, segment 8.

KEY TERMS AND CONCEPTS

advertising
bait-and-switch
behavior control
consumer sovereignty
consumer rights
consumer movement
contributory negligence
corporate (advocacy) advertising
customary pricing
database marketing
deception
deceptive advertising
dependence effect
due care
exclusive dealing
express warranty
fault
Greenman v. *Yuba Power Products*
Henningsen v. *Bloomfield Motors Inc.*
implied warranty of merchantability
implied warranty of fitness for use
invited misuse
lowballing
manipulation
market allocation
marketing concept
negligence
price-fixing
price discrimination
privity
product placement
rational persuasion
rational consumer choice
reasonable consumer standard
reciprocal dealing
resale price maintenance
Robinson-Patman Act
"state-of-the-art" defense
strict liability

subliminal communication
sugging
target marketing
tying arrangements

CHAPTER TWELVE

OCCUPATIONAL HEALTH AND SAFETY

CHAPTER SUMMARY

Chapter 12 addresses employee rights and employer obligations in matters of occupational health and safety by surveying the justification for government regulation of the workplace and of specific regulatory rules and policies. The chapter focuses on three issues: the (legally protected) right of employees to have a safe and healthy workplace, the right to know about workplace hazards, and the right to refuse hazardous work. The chapter concludes with an examination of fetal protection policies as a means for addressing the problem of reproductive hazards in the workplace.

CHAPTER OVERVIEW

Introduction

Employees have a right to be protected from hazardous working conditions that can cause injuries or disease, but questions remains about the appropriate level of safety, the trade-off between safety and cost, and the means for achieving safety. How safe is safe? And how much should employers be required to spend on safety? These questions raise further questions about the use of cost-benefit analysis and market mechanisms for determining levels of safety. Thus, should employees be allowed to bargain over safety and accept dangerous work in return for higher pay? The right of employees to receive information about workplace hazards involves a complex set of questions about the meaning of this right (When have workers been adequately informed?) and its justification (Why is it not sufficient for employers to provide adequate protection?). Additionally, the right to refuse to perform dangerous work requires us to determine the conditions for the exercise of this right. The main question about fetal protection policies is whether they constitute (illegal) sexual discrimination.

The Scope of the Problem

Safety hazards involve workplace conditions that are capable of causing sudden injury, whereas *health hazards* are factors in the workplace that cause illness and other conditions over a lifetime of exposure. The courts do not generally hold employers responsible for occupational diseases (and only recently has workers' compensation recognized them) due to their delayed onset, hidden causal connection, multiplicity of causes, and lack of available information on the diseases. Occupational health and safety was regulated primarily by state governments until the federal government assumed responsibility after the establishment of the *Occupational Safety and Health Administration (OSHA)* with the passage of the *Occupational Safety and Health Act* in 1970 (OSH Act). Although states still play a major role in occupational health and safety through workers' compensation systems, OSHA regulates occupational safety and health mainly by imposing: (1) a *general duty* on employers to furnish employment that is free from recognized hazards that are causing or likely to cause death or serious injury, and (2) a *specific duty* to comply with all the occupational health and safety standards created by OSHA. Examples of standards include *permissible exposure limits (PEL)* for toxic substances and *specifications* for equipment and facilities. Employees also have a duty to adhere to all standards, rules, regulations, and orders issued pursuant to the OSH Act.

The Right to a Safe and Healthy Workplace

An employees' right to a safe and healthy workplace and the corresponding obligation of employers to provide working conditions free from recognized hazards follow, according to some writers, from a fundamental right of survival. Other writers base the right to a safe workplace on the Kantian ground that persons ought to be treated as ends rather than means. Congress employed utilitarian reasoning in passing the OSH Act by balancing the cost to industry with savings to the economy as a whole through cost-benefit analysis. Common law recognizes the right of workers to be protected against harm resulting directly from the actions and fault of employers, but employers can defend themselves against charges of violating workers' rights by arguing that their actions were not the *direct cause* of the death or injury or that the worker *voluntarily assumed the risk.*

The notion of a direct cause. Two factors enable employers to deny they are responsible for a workplace accident. First, they can claim that the accident was caused by a combination of circumstances (*multiplicity of causes*), which may include the actions of the workers themselves. (The law recognizes the role of employees in the common-law defenses of *contributory negligence* and the *fellow-servant rule*.) Second, they can claim that it is not practical to reduce the probability of harm any further. In determining whether the reduction of risk is reasonable, OSHA considers the degree of risk, the availability of substitutes, the benefit of continued risk, and the adequacy of existing controls. These and other issues are at stake in the benzene case (see *Case 12.1 The Regulation of Benzene*).

The voluntary assumption of risk. *The voluntary assumption of risk* limits employer responsibility for employees' injuries on the grounds that employees have freely assumed the risks of a job, often in return for higher wages. Because the assumption of risk is held to be voluntary, some hold that government regulation of occupational health and safety interferes with the freedom of individuals to choose the appropriate level of risk, whereas others are concerned that the risk is not voluntarily assumed but forced on workers. In any event, workers cannot be said to assume the risk of dangerous work when they are unaware of the risks or are unable to bargain for safer working conditions.

Risk and coercion. The concept of *coercion* determines whether workers assume the risk of employment by free choice. A standard analysis of coercion involves getting a person to choose an alternative that he or she does not want and issuing a threat to make the person worse off if he or she does not choose the alternative. On this analysis, whether a person has been coerced depends on what it means to be *worse off*. Robert Nozick and others propose that to be made *worse off* means to be treated in a way that falls below what is morally required. That is, a threat is coercive if the threat is to treat a person in a way that is morally wrong. Accordingly, whether a person is coerced into accepting dangerous work depends on the level of safety that an employer is obligated to provide.

The Right to Know About and Refuse Hazardous Work

Many American workers face the cruel dilemma of being forced to choose between performing hazardous work and suffering disciplinary action. Many people believe that this choice between safety and employment is unjust and that employees ought to be able to refuse orders to perform hazardous work without fear of adverse consequences. Even worse are situations in which workers are unable to take steps to protect themselves because they face hazards of which they are unaware.

Features of the right to know and refuse. Although the *right to refuse hazardous work* is different from the right to a safe and healthy workplace, it is one of several alternatives that workers have for securing a safe and healthy workplace. An employee's *right to know information about hazards* is an aggregation of four rights that may be classified by the correlative duties that they impose on employers. They are the *duty to reveal information* already possessed; the *duty to communicate information* about hazards through labeling, postings, and training programs; the *duty to seek out existing information* from scientific literature or other sources; and the *duty to produce new information* relevant to employee health. Steps to inform workers of hazards are known collectively as *worker notification*, and controversy exists over various proposals for worker notification.

The main argument for denying workers the right to refuse hazardous work is that such a right conflicts with the obligation of employees to obey all *reasonable directives* from an employer. A common-law principle is that employees should obey even an improper order and seek recourse afterward. Employees may be mistaken about the presence of hazards, and chaos would result if they could stop work in the belief that a hazard is present. The flaw in this argument is that later may be too late. Therefore, the right to refuse hazardous work may be necessary to prevent serious injury and even death.

In the Whirlpool case, the Supreme Court cited the following two factors as relevant for justifying a refusal to work: The employee believes in good faith that the working conditions pose an imminent risk of death or serious injury and that the risk cannot be avoided by any less disruptive course of action. The good faith requirement helps to exclude employee refusals based on false charges and sabotage. The three standards commonly used for determining whether good faith refusals are justified are:

1. The *subjective standard*, which requires only that employees demonstrate they sincerely believe a hazard exists.
2. The *objective standard*, which requires that experts identify a hazard exists.
3. The *reasonable person standard*, which requires that the evidence be strong enough to persuade a reasonable person that a hazard exists.

The subjective standard provides the greatest protection for worker health and safety, but to allow workers to shut down production based on their uninformed judgment — versus the informed judgment of management — is likely to result in many costly mistakes. The subjective standard also creates no incentive for workers to be cautious in refusing work because the cost is borne solely by the company. In contrast, the objective standard forces employees to bear the consequences if their beliefs about workplace conditions are groundless. Therefore, the reasonable person standard, which places a moderate burden of proof on employees, is the best balance of the competing considerations.

The justification of a right to know. The right to know about workplace hazards is not necessary for the right to a safe and healthy workplace because the latter right is fully protected if the employer rids the workplace of significant hazards. However, some consider the right to know an effective means for securing the right to a safe workplace, while others believe employees have the right to know independently of the right to a safe workplace.

The most common argument for the right to know is based on *autonomy* and holds that workers can be autonomous only if they possess relevant information, such as the hazards in matters of risk assumption. Employers who maintain that they can protect workers from hazards more effectively than the workers themselves without informing them of the hazards are taking a paternalistic approach that is incompatible with a respect for autonomy. An alternative to informing employees that still respects autonomy is to allow bargaining over information. This alternative is impractical because: (1) it creates a disincentive for employers to yield the information without concessions from employees, (2) there is no basis for determining the value of the information without a ready market, and (3) the transaction costs in the bargaining process are apt to be high.

Two utilitarian arguments for the right to know are that workers who are aware of hazards in the workplace are (1) better equipped to protect themselves and (2) better able to bargain or make rational choices in the job market. The second argument assumes that the level of safety should be determined by market forces, but these forces can operate only if employees are aware of the risks. Although these two utilitarian arguments provide strong support for the right to know, other means of securing worker health and safety, such as government regulation, might be more efficient. Employees' right to know about workplace hazards may conflict with the employers' right to protect trade secrets, but both rights may be preserved in a number of ways, such as revealing the information about hazards without revealing the more critical trade secret information or by revealing the information to union representatives or an employee's own doctor under a pledge of confidentiality.

The Problem of Reproductive Hazards.

What steps should employers take to protect the health of the fetus of a pregnant employee? In 1977, Johnson Controls, Inc., manufacturer of lead batteries, answered this question by requiring women to sign a statement that they had been told of the risks associated with having a child while exposed to lead in the workplace. However, when some women became pregnant with high lead blood levels, the company adopted a fetal protection policy that excluded all women of childbearing age from all jobs where lead is present. In April 1984, a class action suit was filed charging that Johnson Control's fetal protection policy violated the Title VII prohibition against sex discrimination.

Aside from the charge of discrimination, fetal protection policies raise two other questions. First, who decides? In adopting a fetal protection policy, managers assume the right to decide how a fetus will be protected, but because women employees bear the cost, they contend that they have the right to make this decision. Second, critics claim that companies that exclude fertile women from jobs effectively force sterilization on those who have no other satisfactory employment opportunities.

Issues in the charge of sex discrimination. It is discriminatory for employers to adopt a fetal protection policy that applies only to women and not to men if men are vulnerable as well. Fetal protection policies are also discriminatory if they are applied only to women who occupy traditionally male jobs and not to women in female-dominated lines of work, such as nurses, x-ray technicians, and dry-cleaning employees, who also face reproductive hazards. Critics contend that fetal protection policies have been used to reinforce job segregation through selective application to women in areas formerly dominated by men.

Title VII provides employers with two defenses to charges of sex discrimination: the *business necessity* defense (in which a policy that excludes one sex serves a legitimate business purpose) and the *BFOQ* defense (in which a person's sex is a bona fide occupational qualification). In the *Johnson Controls* case, the lower courts ruled that the fetal protection policy was permissible on the basis of both defenses, but the U.S. Supreme Court over-ruled the lower courts and held Johnson Control's fetal protection policy to be discriminatory in violation of Title VII. The high court ruled that because fetal protection policies constitute disparate treatment and not merely disparate impact [see Chapter 8 for the distinction], only the BFOQ defense is permitted. The courts ruled further that being a man is not a BFOQ for battery making because women are able to make batteries as well as men and because a fetus is not endangered by the manner in which the job is performed.

Two issues remain: how best to protect a fetus from hazards in the workplace and how to protect employers from possibly ruinous liability suits for prenatal injuries. The *Johnson Controls* decision leaves the welfare of future children in the hands of parents who, the court contend, have a more compelling interest in their children's welfare than employers. The court also expressed the view that the possibility of heavy tort liability against employers is "remote at best" if they (1) fully inform employees of the risks and (2) do not act negligently.

CASE SUMMARIES

Case 12.1 The Regulation of Benzene

In 1977, OSHA declared benzene to be a leukemia-causing agent and issued an emergency temporary standard ordering that the permissible exposure limit (PEL) be reduced from 10 parts per million (ppm) to 1 ppm until a hearing could be conducted. The basis for this decision was a law that requires the PEL for a known carcinogen be set at the lowest technologically feasible level that will not impair the viability of the industries being regulated. The American Petroleum Institute contended in a lawsuit that the evidence linking benzene to leukemia was not conclusive and that the exposure standard should take into account the cost of compliance. [Postscript: The Supreme Court struck down the 1 ppm standard because the agency was unable to prove that exposure to benzene below 10 ppm is harmful. In March 1986, OSHA announced a new standard based on subsequent research that set PEL at 1 ppm (or 5 ppm for short-term exposure), but by this time the industry had already reduced the level of exposure to 1 ppm.]

Discussion Questions

1. How much evidence should OSHA have for setting PELs? Is merely some evidence sufficient, or should the agency have conclusive proof? Would your answer to this question depend on the severity of the harm involved? That is, should less evidence be required for a suspected carcinogen?

2. Should the cost of complying with a standard be taken into consideration? Would your answer to this question or the previous question change if you knew that a safe, inexpensive substitute was available?

Case Objectives

The benzene case provides an example of a hazardous substance that is subject to OSHA regulation and raises questions about the setting of OSHA standards. Specifically, should the standards consider the amount of evidence available and the cost of compliance? Although Benzene is clearly a hazardous substance, some instructors may want to use this example to ask whether such substances should be subject to government regulation, or whether employees should be informed when they are exposed to benzene or other toxic chemicals within the permissible limit.

Case 12.2 Whirlpool Corporation

Two employees at a Whirlpool plant in Marion, Ohio, were ordered to perform maintenance work on overhead conveyers that carried components for the assembly of household appliances. The two employees, Virgil Deemer and Thomas Cornwell, believed the work to be unsafe and refused to perform the work. Although a screen had been constructed underneath the conveyors, several employees had fallen through the screen, one to his death. Deemer and Cornwell had expressed their concerns to their supervisor and the plant safety director, and Deemer had consulted with the a local OSHA representative. Because of the refusal to perform the work, the two employees lost six hours wages after being ordered to punch out, and written reprimands were placed in their personnel files.

Discussion Questions

1. Were Deemer and Cornwell justified in their actions? Do they have a right to refuse to do the work that they were ordered to do? What is the basis and justification for such a refusal?
2. Were Deemer and Cornwell justified in their belief that the work is hazardous? What condition must their belief meet in order for their refusal to be justified? Suppose, for example, that Deemer and Cornwell were sincere in their belief but that most experts would believe the work to be safe, or that most reasonable persons would belief the work to be safe. Would they still be justified in refusing to perform the work?
3. Could Deemer and Cornwell have protected themselves in some other way? If so, would their refusal to perform the work still be justified?

Case Objectives

The case illustrates the main issues surrounding the claim of an employee's right to refuse to do hazardous work. In particular, the case can be used to explain and assess the framework developed by the Supreme Court in *Whirlpool Corporation v. Marshall*, namely that (1) the employee reasonably believes the working conditions pose an imminent risk of serious injury or death and (2) the employee believes that the risk cannot be avoided by less disruptive means. The pivotal question is, what is the standard for reasonable belief? Through discussion, the instructor can explore the subjective, objective, and reasonable person standards.

Case 12.3 Johnson Controls, Inc.

In 1982, Johnson Controls, a manufacturer of lead batteries, adopted a fetal protection policy that excluded fertile women from jobs that involved exposure to lead, which is know to harm a developing fetus. In 1984, a group of workers filed a class action suit charging that the fetal protection policy was illegal sex discrimination under Title VII of the 1964 Civil Rights Act. Previously, the company had warned women about the dangers of lead and required them to sign a statement that they understood the dangers, but these measures had not prevented eight women from becoming pregnant with dangerously high levels of lead in their blood. OSHA recommended that women who planned to conceive maintain low levels of lead in their blood, but the agency concluded that there was no reason to remove women from jobs involving lead exposure.

Discussion Questions

1. Is Johnson Control's fetal protection policy well-formulated? Specifically, is the wording that excludes "women who are capable of bearing children" too broad? Could this statement be made narrower without adverse consequences? (Note: if the policy excluded women who were not sexually active or who were practicing adequate birth control, then the policy might invade their privacy.)
2. Should the policy exclude women "whose inability to bear children is medically documented"? Could the failure to include this exception be justified? Does including it coerce women into undergoing surgical sterilization?
3. What reasons led Johnson Controls to adopt the fetal protection policy? Are these legitimate reasons? What could be the consequences if the company had failed to take some measures to protect women from lead exposure? (Note: the company has an obligation not only to employees to provide a safe and healthy workplace but also to shareholders to protect the company against legal liability.)
4. Is the fetal protection policy discriminatory? How could a lawyer for the plaintiffs argue in court?
5. Are there less discriminatory ways of addressing the problem? What other solutions might the company have adopted? (Note: the courts generally hold that a practice is discriminatory if a less discriminatory alternative is available.)
6. Is the inability to become pregnant a BFOQ?
7. Is the Supreme Court decision sound public policy? Is the legal prohibition against fetal protection policies acceptable from the point of view of both employers and employees?

Case Objectives

First, the case provides a good example of conflict between two important obligations, namely the obligations not to discriminate and to provide a safe and healthy workplace. Reconciling these two obligations presents a difficult managerial dilemma. Second, the case presents another context in which to discuss features of Title VII discrimination law and in particular the interpretation of the BFOQ defense. Third, the case raises a possible conflict between deciding issues on narrow legal grounds and considering broader issues of public policy. Aside from validity of the legal reasoning, discussion should focus on whether the decision in *Johnson Controls* is good social policy and whether companies should take public policy into account in formulating their own policies.

Case 12.4 Employees as Guinea Pigs

Many companies, especially auto-makers and consumer-product companies, use employees for product testing. In a test of the evacuation slide of a new jetliner, 50 McDonnell Douglas employees were injured, some seriously. Although employees volunteer for such testing, some critics suggest that the practice of using employees for product testing creates subtle pressure. Other critics argue that injuries can lead to low morale and that workers may be poor test participants due to their lack of objectivity. Supporters of the practice reply that employees have an interest in improving products and are eager to participate beyond their job function.

Discussion Questions

1. Is the practice of using employees for product testing a good idea? Should this question be decided merely by comparing the advantages and disadvantages to the company and to employees? (Note that testing with human subjects creates safer products for consumers and, in some instances, is required by law.)

2. Does it matter whether the test subjects are employees or other people? Does the practice of using employees for product testing raise any issues that would not arise if test subjects were volunteers from the community, or if testing was conducted with professional testers?

3. If employees volunteer, can they be said to have assumed the risk if they are seriously injured in an accident?

4. Could the test that was conducted by McDonnell Douglas be said to constitute a hazardous workplace? If so, can the practice of using employees for product testing be reconciled with the OSHA general duty to provide employees with a workplace "free from recognized hazards that are causing or likely to cause death or serious injury?"

Case Objectives

This case provides an opportunity to apply the concepts of direct cause, assumption of the risk, and coercion as they apply to a hazardous workplace. Using employees as test subjects exposes them to risks that are not part of their job function and that can be easily avoided. Although only volunteers are used for product testing, the possibility of coercion brings the voluntariness of the employees' participation into doubt. If the advantages and disadvantages are compared, the instructor can ask whether these advantages and disadvantages are fairly distributed between employers and employees. Employees may derive some benefits, but the practice appears to occur mainly for the convenience of the employers. Finally, the instructor might ask students to consider whether this practice is an effective form of testing and whether the whole of society is best served by it.

TEACHING STRATEGIES

1. Genetic screening, which is discussed only briefly in the textbook, is a controversial practice that some instructors might want to explore at greater length. An in-depth study by a sociologist that also considers reproductive hazards and fetal protection policies is Elaine Draper, *Risky Business:*

Genetic Testing and Exclusionary Practices in the Hazardous Workplace (Cambridge: Cambridge University Press, 1991).

2. Ask the class as a group or individually to develop a right-to-know policy for a company and, in particular, to identify the specific issues that such a policy should address. Alternatively, students can be asked to analyze the case "Responding to a Sweeping Right-to-Know Proposal" in *Cases in Ethics and the Conduct of Business* and to list the issues raised by the writers of the memos in the case. The case provides an opportunity to examine issues of employee health and safety from the perspective of different managerial functions (labor relations, public relations, and manufacturing) and to explore issues in lobbying government to secure favorable health and safety regulation.

3. Invite a health and safety expert from a local company to give a presentation. Many manufacturing and industrial companies have developed comprehensive, state-of-the-art programs which they are proud to present to the public, and some speakers may be willing to share difficult health and safety problems that their company has encountered.

4. The ABC News / Prentice Hall Video Library includes a 50-minute ABC Special "Working in America: Hazardous Duty" that vividly illustrates dangers in the workplace and the problems of regulation. Another video, "Women in Hazardous Jobs" is available from Prentice Hall, College Division Video Catalog.

KEY TERMS AND CONCEPTS

bona fide occupational qualification (BFOQ)
business necessity
coercion
contributory negligence
direct cause
fellow-servant rule
fetal protection policy
fetotoxins, teratogens, mutagens
general duty clause
multiplicity of causes
National Institute of Occupational Safety and
      Health (NIOSH)
Occupational Safety and Health Administration   (OSHA)
Occupational Safety and Health Act of 1970
      (OSH Act)
permissible exposure limit (PEL)
reasonable belief
reproductive hazards
right-to-know
safety and health hazards
specific duties

subjective / objective / reasonable person
      standard
technological feasibility
trade secrets
voluntary assumption of the risk
worker notification

CHAPTER THIRTEEN

ETHICS AND CORPORATIONS

CHAPTER SUMMARY

Corporations have responsibilities to many groups, including *employees, suppliers, customers*, and *communities*. Disagreements inevitably arise regarding the exact responsibilities corporations have toward each of these constituencies as well as about the meaning of the concept of corporate social responsibility. The first section of this chapter examines the commonly accepted understanding of corporate social responsibility and compares it to the classical view of corporations, with special attention to the arguments of Milton Friedman. The second section discusses the arguments for shareholder control of corporations, specifically the property rights, social institution, and contractual arguments. Stakeholder theory is presented and criticized as an alternative to shareholder control. The third section describes the efforts of corporations to institutionalize ethics by means of ethics programs.

CHAPTER OVERVIEW

The concept of corporate social responsibility originated in the 1950s, as American corporations rapidly increased in size and power. The topic continued to wield influence in public debates during the sixties and seventies as the nation confronted pressing social problems such as poverty, unemployment, and pollution. Although there are varying interpretations of social responsibility, the standard view recognizes that business firms have two main sets of responsibilities. Corporations have *economic* responsibilities to produce goods and services, to provide jobs and good wages to the workforce, to seek out supplies of raw materials, to improve technology, and to develop new products—all the while making a profit. Corporations also have many *legal* responsibilities that are set forth in the voluminous body of business law.

Corporate Social Responsibility

Social responsibility is the selection and evaluation of corporate goals based not only on profitability and organizational well-being, but also on ethical standards of social desirability. Archie B. Carroll describes corporate social responsibility as a four stage continuum that includes, beyond economic and legal responsibility, ethical conduct that is expected but not legally required of business and responsibilities that corporations voluntarily accept. The 1971 Committee for Economic Development report characterized corporate social responsibility as three concentric circles. The inner circle included the clear-cut basic responsibilities for the efficient execution of a corporation's economic function: products, jobs, and economic growth. The intermediate circle encompassed a company's responsibility to exercise this economic function with an awareness of changing social values and priorities through environmental awareness, employee relations, information availability, and safety. The outer circle outlined new responsibilities that addressed such major social problems as poverty and urban blight. Corporations have considerable resources for solving these problems.

Finally, S. Prakash Sethi argues that corporate social responsibility is behavior that is necessary for corporations to gain legitimacy and thus consists of "bringing corporate behavior up to a level where it is congruent with prevailing social norms, values, and expectations of performance."

There are various types of corporate activities that exhibit corporate responsibility. They include choosing to operate the corporation on a level higher than the law requires, contributing to civic, charitable, and nonprofit institutions, providing benefits to employees and improving the quality of the workplace, taking advantage of an economic opportunity that is less profitable but more socially desirable, and using corporate resources to address some major social problem. None of these activities is necessarily antithetical to corporate interests or even the long term profitability of a corporation, and some of the most successful corporations are also among the most socially responsible.

Another important aspect of corporate responsibility is *responsiveness*, which, according to William C. Frederick, is a company's ability to respond to new challenges. The management of social issues in a socially responsive corporation is integrated into the strategic planning process instead of being handled as an *ad hoc* reaction to specific crises. A shortcoming of the concept of social responsiveness is that it does not specify how a corporation should respond to actual social issues. One suggestion, by Donna Wood, is that responsiveness be understood as a configuration of *principles*, *processes*, *policies*, and *observable outcomes*.

The Classical View. The major challenge to the idea that corporations should be socially responsible comes from the classical view of corporate social responsibility that prevailed in the nineteenth century and is common among economists. This view consists of three basic propositions.

1. Economic behavior is separate and distinct from other types of behavior. Thus businesses do not have the same goals as other organizations in society.
2. The primary criteria of business performance are economic efficiency, growth in the production of goods and services, technological development, and innovation in goods and services.
3. The primary goal and motivation of business is profit.

Among the problems with the classical view are the following.

1. *The moral minimum of the market.* The classical view does not adequately appreciate the extent to which social responsibility is required by free markets. The claim that a business must choose between either getting involved in the management of society or fulfilling the profit-making function excludes another possible role of corporate responsibility, namely making profits in a manner that minimizes social injury. Although not all corporations have an *affirmative duty* to take on specific tasks, all are under a *negative injunction* to prevent specific harms from occurring. If the minimum level of conduct is whatever the law requires, then corporations leave themselves open to intervention by external forces, including pressure from special interest groups and government regulation. But by *internalizing* the expectations of society, corporations can retain control over decision making and avoid the costs associated with government regulation.

2. *Power and responsibility.* Because corporations have become so large and powerful, they are not effectively restrained by market forces and government regulation and as such, some self-imposed restraint is needed. The social responsibility of corporations thus arises from their new social power. Keith Davis expresses this view as the Iron Law of Responsibility: "In the long run, those who do not use power in a manner which society considers responsible will tend to lose it." To the charge that it would be dangerous to release the immense power of corporations from the discipline of the market, defenders of corporate social responsibility argue that the decision by a corporation not to exercise its economic influence is itself a moral decision that affects the community.

3. *Giving a helping hand to government.* Third, the classical view justifies its distinction between the proper spheres of activity for business and government on the grounds of utilitarian efficiency. But although certain non-economic goals are better left to government, it does not follow that corporations have no obligation to provide a helping hand. Four criteria can be used to determine whether corporations have an obligation to pursue noneconomic goals. They are the *urgency* of the need, the *proximity* of the corporation to the need, the *capability* of a corporation to respond effectively, and the likelihood that the *need* will not be met unless a corporation acts.

Friedman's Arguments against Social Responsibility. Milton Friedman holds that corporate officials have no social responsibility beyond serving the interests of their stockholders. His main argument is that a corporate executive has no right to spend someone else's money—the stockholder's, customer's or employee's—for a general social interest. This does not mean that corporations ought to be permitted to act irresponsibly. Friedman himself acknowledges that business must observe certain limitations on conduct, which he describes as the *rules of the game*, and some government is necessary to enforce these rules. However, it is the job of society to establish a framework of law such that corporations will serve society by seeking profit within the rules of the game. The classical view does not sanction an unrestrained pursuit of profit. Friedman also recognizes that many socially responsible actions serve the corporation's own interest, and he considers these to be legitimate as long as the actions ultimately benefit the shareholders and are not purely philanthropic.

Holders of the classical view generally admit the legitimacy of three functions of government with regard to business:

1. Business activity generates many externalities or social harms (such as pollution and worker injury) that governments may force business to internalize.

2. The operation of a free market results in considerable inequalities in the distribution of income and wealth, and it is the job of government to manage the equity/efficiency trade-off.

3. Free markets are prone to instability that manifests itself in inflation, recession, and unemployment, and government should use its powers of taxation, public expenditure, and control of the money supply to stabilize the economy.

According to the taxation argument, all profits of a corporation belong to the shareholders, so that corporate managers who spend money for social causes are taxing the shareholders and distributing the proceeds. In so doing, managers are exceeding their authority and assuming the powers of government. Advocates of corporate social responsibility argue in reply that although shareholders have well-defined legal rights, many other groups have both moral and legal claims that compete with those of shareholders. Specifically:

1. *The question of means.* Though managers are obligated to earn a profit for shareholders, they are not morally permitted to do so by any means possible. Although Friedman recognizes limits in the "rules of the game," these may be more extensive than the minimal rules that he lists.

2. *Taking a long-term view.* Earning a maximum return for shareholders in the long run requires corporations to act in a socially responsible manner and to satisfy the legitimate expectations of society. One problem, however, is determining how much socially responsible behavior is in a corporation's long-term self-interest.

3. *What are the interests of shareholders?* Some object that managers are often more profit-minded than the shareholders themselves. Because shareholders are consumers, citizens of communities, and even environmentalists, they may, in fact, favor a certain amount of socially responsible conduct by corporations. Friedman might respond that shareholders who favor certain social goals can use their dividends for that purpose. However, it may be more efficient for corporations to expend funds on environmental protection, for example, than for shareholders to spend the same amount in dividends for the same purpose.

Corporate Governance

Deciding how corporations ought to be governed involves some answer to the questions, in whose interests should corporations be run? In answering this question, the law on corporate governance has drawn on three theories about the nature of the corporation: the property rights theory, the social institution theory, and the contractual theory.

The Property Rights and Social Institution Theories. The property rights theory views the corporation as a *private* entity, in which individuals exercise their property rights and right of contract to pool their assets to do business in the corporate form. By contrast, the social institution theory regards the corporation as a *public* entity, in which the state grants individuals the right to do business in the corporate form in order to serve some social good. The court opinion in *Dodge* v. *Ford Motor Co.* expresses the property rights theory by holding that shareholders, as owners of the corporation, have a right that it be operated solely in their interests.

The property rights theory, which is assumed in the *Dodge* decision, was undermined by the development of the separation of ownership and control, which was documented by Adolf Berle and Gardiner Means in *The Modern Corporation and Private Property* (1932). Berle and Means argued that shareholders were no longer owners in any meaningful sense and so had lost any claim that the corporation be run in their interests.

Merrick Dodd argued that because shareholders no longer had a claim based on property rights, corporations had become public institutions that ought to be run in the interests of all groups in society. Berle disagreed on the grounds that Dodd's proposal, if implemented, would leave the power of managers without any effective restraint. Berle argued that managers ought to run corporations in the interests of shareholders, not because the shareholders deserved this as owners–because they had ceased to be owners–but because everyone else would benefit by this effective check on managerial power. The court opinion in *A. P. Smith Manufacturing* v. *Barlow* departed from the precedent set in the *Dodge* and reflected Dodd's position.

The Contractual Theory. On the contractual theory, the firm is a nexus of contracts among all of its constituencies, in which groups deploy their economic assets for some return. Each group incurs some risk when these assets are firm-specific, but in general this risk is reduced by contracts that provide adequate protection. For example, employees who develop firm-specific skills may protect themselves with contracts that guarantee secure employment. The role of shareholders in a firm is to provide capital in return for a claim on the residual, that is the revenues that remain after all other obligations (such as wages to employees and payments to creditors) have been met. Shareholders thus bear the preponderance of residual risk, which is to say that they are the first to bear any loss suffered by the firm.

Control rights–that is the right of a group to control the corporation so that it is run in that group's interest–can be sought by any group, and in some instances control may be held by employees, suppliers, or customers. However, most publicly-held companies in the United States are controlled by shareholders. On the contractual theory, shareholder control is the result of bargaining among all corporate constituencies.

The main argument for shareholder control is that corporations are most run most efficiently when they are controlled by residual risk bearers. The reason is that if other groups had control, they would run the corporation with a view to remaining solvent, that is generating sufficient revenues to meet all fixed claims of employees, creditors, etc. Only residual risk bearers stand to benefit if the corporation is run to maximize revenues, because they have a claim on all residual revenues. However, everyone ultimately benefits if corporations create the maximum of wealth.

The contractual theory is subject to four objections.

1. *Externalities.* Serving the interests of shareholders alone may lead corporations to impose externalities, such as pollution, on society. The contractual theory response is to deny that problems like pollution are due to shareholder control and to seek other kinds of solutions.
2. *Implicit Contracts.* Service the interests of shareholders alone may lead corporations to breach implicit contracts with employees and other groups. Response: Implicit contracts may better serve the interests of nonshareholder constituencies, even though they can often be breachedwithout legal consequences. For example, the stronger job guarantees of European workers deprive employers the freedom to undertake changes that in the long run create more employment and higher wages. In some instances, the law creates legally binding obligations that prevent corporations from breaching implicit contracts.
3. *Residual Risk.* Not all residual risk is borne by shareholders, and so the logic of the argument for shareholder control would entail that some control rights should go to nonshareholder constituencies. Response: On the contractual theory, control can and often will be shared. For example, employees who bear residual risk are sometimes compensated in stock and stock options.
4. *Distribution and Power.* Insofar as the contractual theory assumes bargaining among all corporate constituencies, an unequal distribution of wealth and power may result in unequal outcomes in corporate governance. Response: This is true, but the problem cannot be corrected by

changing corporate governance but only by social and political change. For example, some legislation, such as labor law, is intended to correct inequalities in bargaining power.

The stakeholder theory. Under this view, instead of serving the interests of only shareholders or stockholders, corporations ought to be operated for the benefit of all those who have a stake in the enterprise. A *stakeholder* is usually defined as any group that is vital to the success of the corporation, and the most frequently mentioned stakeholder groups are investors, employees, customers, suppliers, and the local community. Critics of stakeholder theory agree that these groups have interests but deny that the corporation is morally obligated to take them into account merely because they affect a firm. Rather, corporations have an obligation only to respect the *rights* of each stakeholder group within the rules of market exchanges.

Thomas Donaldson and Lee Preston have identified three uses of the stakeholder model:

1. *Descriptive.* A researcher who believes that the stakeholder model accurately *describes* corporations can use it to answer questions about how corporations are organized and managed. It can also be used to evaluate what people in corporations think about their roles.
2. *Instrumental.* The stakeholder model can be used *instrumentally*, as a tool for managers, and telling managers to handle stakeholder relations well may be a more practical action guide than aiming at profit directly.
3. *Normative.* Stakeholder theory can be used *normatively*, as an account of how corporations ought to treat various stakeholder groups. The theory holds that the interests of all groups are of intrinsic value and worth furthering for their own sake.

Among critics of stakeholder theory, Igor Ansoff argues that responsibilities to stakeholders are not objectives of a corporation but constraints on the pursuit of its objectives, one of which is to operate at a profit. Kenneth Goodpaster argues that the responsibility of a manager to shareholders is different from the responsibility to other stakeholder groups because the managers have a *fiduciary duty* to shareholders, whereas the obligations to employees, customers, and others are nonfiduciary in character. Finally, some critics charge that stakeholder theory fails as a *decision-making guide* for business. Many corporate decisions involve trade-offs in which the benefits of one group must be balanced against the losses of another, and the theory gives little guidance for managing such trade-offs.

Corporate Ethics Programs

Many U.S. and some foreign corporations have established corporate ethics programs that are intended both to guide individual conduct and to shape the corporate environment. The components of ethics programs typically include a code of ethics, ethics training, communication with employees, and some mechanism for reporting, investigating, and correcting wrongdoing.

The main benefits of an ethics program are: (a) reducing the risk of losses from wrongdoing, (b) enabling organizational change, (c) managing external relations, and (d) fulfilling obligations to shareholders. Note: the establishment of an ethics program has become a part of the obligation to serve shareholder interests as a result of the *Caremark* opinion and the Federal Sentencing Guidelines.

The Federal Sentencing Guidelines are important for the development of ethics programs because the existence of an effective program result in a more lenient sentence for an organization convicted of a crime. The guidelines also present criteria for determining whether an ethics program is effective.

CASE SUMMARIES

Case 13.1 Campbell Soup Company

In 1985, the Campbell Soup Company faced a challenge from a group called the Farm Labor Organizing Committee (FLOC) which was fighting for increased wages and improved living and working conditions for migrant farm workers in Ohio. Since 1979 the company had been the target of a nationwide boycott of its products, instigated by FLOC and supported by Ohio church groups. At the urging of the National Council of Churches, which had been persuaded by FLOC to intervene in the dispute, the two sides agreed on a vote to determine whether the farm workers wanted to be represented by FLOC. The election process broke down, however, amid allegations by FLOC of unfair labor practices, including charges that the growers brought in local laborers on the day of the election and prevented some migrant farm workers from voting. Although Campbell had taken many steps to address the plight of migrant farm workers, support for the boycott continued to build. The National Council of Churches set a deadline for a new agreement and threatened to back the boycott if the deadline was not met. R. Gordon McGovern, the president and CEO of Campbell, believed that the company had met its obligations to the migrant farm workers but faced a decision on how to respond to these developments.

Discussion Questions

1. Is the plight of the migrant farm workers a social problem that ought to be addressed? Why did this problem become the concern of church groups?
2. Why did FLOC target Campbell in their attempt to form a union? Was it fair for FLOC to target the company?
3. What is Campbell's responsibility for addressing this problem? Is Campbell in any way responsible for this problem? Can this problem be solved without Campbell's involvement? (Hint: use the four criteria of urgency, proximity, capability, and a need for corporate assistance.)
4. What should Campbell's objective be in responding to the threat of a national boycott backed by the National Council of Churches? How should Campbell respond?

Case Objectives

The Campbell Soup case describes a difficult period in which company executives were forced to determine the extent of their responsibility to a stakeholder group that was applying great pressure on the company. A fuller version of this case appears in *Cases in Ethics and the Conduct of Business*.

Although the plight of the migrant farm workers is a social problem that ought to be addressed by someone (as evidenced by the involvement of church groups), the obligation of Campbell to address the problem is not clear. Ordinarily, a company is not responsible for the employees of a supplier, but in this case the growers are not wholly independent of Campbell (the company provided seedlings to the growers and had ordered the growers to switch to mechanical harvesters in response to a strike in 1978). The court case which addressed the issue of child labor considered the farm workers in pickle fields to be independent contractors rather than employees, in which case the responsibility of Campbell would be less. So students might be asked to consider whether the farm workers are employees or independent contractors and what difference the distinction makes.

Furthermore, Campbell holds the key to any solution to the problem, in part because the price that the company set for tomatoes did not allow enough profit margin for the growers to increase wages and improve working conditions. It should be noted that this is a typical labor-management dispute that in any other industry could be settled under the National Labor Relations Act, but when this act was passed in 1935, farm laborers were deliberately excluded. Thus, Campbell is being called upon to exercise social responsibility because of the lack of a legal framework for dispute resolution.

Corporate social responsibility is often regarded as voluntary behavior by a corporation, but in this case Campbell must act in order to avoid a nationwide boycott backed by a powerful church group. Regardless of whether Campbell executives believe that they have a responsibility to the farm workers, they must develop a strategy in an environment in which important stakeholder groups believe that they have such a responsibility. Therefore, any strategy must be perceived as fair by these other groups. In addition, the power of the company to force a solution is limited, and so moral arguments about responsibility become a tool that the company can use in developing an effective strategy. The choices of strategy include attack (all-out war), stonewalling, delay and appeasement, negotiating in good faith, and conceding (give 'em what they want). Discussion can be built around a consideration of each of these strategies.

The outcome was that in February 1986 a three-way agreement was signed by FLOC, Campbell, and the growers that provided improved wages and working conditions for the farm workers and guaranteed markets for the growers. An article, "Campbell Soup Accord Ends a Decade of Strife," *New York Times*, February 24, 1986, describes the agreement. This article can be copied and distributed to students at the end of the discussion. A noteworthy feature of the settlement is that Campbell had to take a leadership role in organizing the growers so that they could be represented in the negotiations.

Case 13.2 Bath Iron Works

Two vice presidents of Bath Iron Works (BIW) discovered a document with confidential information about a competitor's cost analysis on a Defense Department project for which the two companies were bidding. After reviewing the document for fifteen minutes, the CEO William E. Haggett ordered the two executives to make copies and examine it until he returned to make a final decision.

In the meantime, the president of BIW realized that possession of the document was forbidden by the federal Procurement Integrity Act and by the principles of the Defense Industry Initiative. The president orderedhat all copies be destroyed and the executives cease their examination. Upon his return, Haggett agreed that he had made an "inappropriate business-ethics decision." Possession of the document could result in the suspension or debarment of BIW as a defense contractor. The two vice presidents and CEO Haggett were asked to leave the company.

Discussion Questions

1. Is possession of confidential information about a competitor more serious in the case of a defense contractor? What specific features of defense industry contracting would account for the greater seriousness of such possession of confidential information?

2. Principle 4 of the Defense Industry Initiative requires signatories to voluntarily report all violations of federal procurement laws. Why would any defense contractor agree to such a strong requirement?

3. CEO Haggett was forced to end a 28-year association with BIW. Was his "fifteeen minutes of ethical uncertainty" of sufficient seriousness to warrant such an outcome? The other executives were merely following Haggett's instructions. Should they have been asked to resign? (Note: the executives may have gone beyond their orders by examining and modeling the data.)

4. This incident occurred despite an ethics program. Do you think that "beefing up" the ethics program is an effective response to the incident? (Note: this incident is now part of the "folklore" at BIW, which by itself teaches an important ethics "lesson.")

5. Lynn Paine asserts that wrongdoing is seldom the work of a rogue employee but results from the corporate culture. Is this case an illustration or an exception to her claim?

Case Objectives

The BIW case shows that thoughtless actions, no less than deliberate wrongdoing, can inflict great harm on a company. It also illustrates the need for an ethics program to prevent such conduct, while at the same time demonstrating the inadequacy of an ethics program to prevent all misconduct. Thus, the case raises questions about how any company can prevent and respond to wrongdoing. In addition, the BIW case can be used to explore the reasons for the development of the Defense Industry Initiative, which constitutes, in Lynn Paine's terms, an integrity strategy. Why does it make sense for a defense contractor like BIW to employ an integrity strategy rather than a compliance strategy?

Case 13.3 Sears Auto Centers

In 1992, Sears Auto Centers were under investigation in California and several other states for performing unnecessary auto repairs and overcharging. The problems resulted apparently from a new incentive system that included commissions and quotas for service advisers and an hourly rate for mechanics based on the time required to install parts. The incentive system was part of company-wide effort at Sears Roebuck to boost lagging performance in all areas of its business. In the end, Sears eliminated the incentive system and took other measures to settle the legal charges and prevent a recurrence.

Discussion Questions

Incentive systems are common in many retail businesses. How is the system at Sears Auto Centers different from those employed elsewhere? Was it well-designed? What changes would you have recommended?

Sears claimed that the quotas were based on averages, so that they also served as a check on whether advisers were doing their job. Is there anything wrong with this use?

How could the mechanics' compensation scheme encourage them to recommend unnecessary repairs? (Note: As long as there were enough repairs to keep mechanics busy, there was no incentive to recommend unnecessary repairs, but if business was slow, then the mechanics' wages would be lower. Also, the mechanics might be able to work more quickly if they performed unnecessary work on a car that was already being repaired.)

Should a part be replaced only if it has already failed? Was Sears justified in a policy of replacing a part if it was likely to fail? Can such a policy be implemented ethically? (Note: suppose the advisers had explained the policy to customers and given them the choice of which policy to be followed in the repair of their cars. Would this have made a difference?)

Case Objectives

The Sears Auto Centers case is a good example of wrongdoing that results inadvertently from a faulty incentive system. In this respect, it is similar to the lesson of Case 3.3 "An Auditor's Dilemma." On a deeper level, the problem may have also arisen from a lack of oversight and an unrealistic strategic plan to increase revenues. This incident prompted Sears to develop its laudable ethics program, which can be cited in a discussion of how the company should act to prevent a recurrence.

TEACHING STRATEGIES

1. Friedman's arguments against corporate social responsibility usually generate good discussion. Students might be asked whether Friedman's sharp separation of the roles of business and government is realistic. The textbook discussion contends that Friedman's arguments permit much more social activism than Friedman acknowledges. In particular, students should be asked to consider what are the "rules of the game" and what role business plays in creating them. Is it consistent for business leaders to say that their only responsibility is to play by the rules of the game when they also had a large role in creating the rules? Indeed, on Friedman's view, how can businesses be justified in lobbying government at all? Students may also be asked whether corporations can maintain their legitimacy without being socially responsible. Even if Freidman is right, would this matter if society does not accept his argument? For a close analysis of Friedman's arguments see Thomas Carson, "Friedman's Theory of Corporate Social Responsibility," *Business and Professional Ethics Journal*, 12 (1993), 3-32.

2. The literature on stakeholder theory is extensive and expanding. The textbook offers a rather skeptical assessment of stakeholder theory, but more sympathetic instructors may want to give the theory greater prominence in discussions of corporate social responsibility. The basic stakeholder model (shown in Figure 13.2) is a good analytical tool for case discussion. In virtually every case of corporate conduct, it is helpful to ask: Who are the stakeholders? And what is the responsibility of the corporation to each stakeholder group? In many cases, there are "hidden" stakeholders, who are not readily apparent. It is important for students to realize that many cases involve conflicts among stakeholder groups and that corporations are often referees among competing interests. Students may be asked how they would manage the trade-offs that inevitably arise as a result of corporate decisions. For example, increasing the pension benefits of employees might result in higher prices to consumers, or a switch to environmentally safer packaging might lead to the termination of a supplier.

3. Many company's codes are publicly available. Obtain a number of ethics codes and ask students to compare and analyze them. What do the statements leave out? How could the statements be made stronger? Students may also be asked to research specific corporate programs that target social problems. Corporations with prominent ethics programs are often willing to provide other materials that can also be examined in class.

4. Many cases and videos on corporate social responsibility are available. The Business Enterprise Trust has produced a series of cases with accompanying videos that profile outstanding examples of socially responsible individuals and corporations. The story of the clearing of a neighborhood in order to build an automobile plant is told in a provocative 54-minute documentary "Poletown Lives!" and in a 45-minute CBS report "What's Good for GM. . . ." For a contrasting view of an example of social outreach by a company, see "Detroit Auto Workers Adopt Struggling Elementary School," in *ABC News/Prentice Hall Video Library*. A 25-minute video of a discussion of the issues in corporate social responsibility by several experts is "Corporations and Conscience," which is Segment 10 of the *Ethics in Management Video Supplement*, published by the Harvard Business School. The video "Your Job or Mine?" by the University of Michigan School of Business, examines Green Giant's move to Mexico, which is the topic of Case 4.1 in the textbook, "Green Giant Runs for the Border." Two other cases on corporate social responsibility in *Cases in Ethics and the Conduct of Business* are "ABC Corporation and Employment Stabilization," and "Chemical Bank: Corporate Contributions."

5. The section on corporate governance is a good springboard for discussing the topic of corporate takeovers. An excellent video for this purpose is "Anatomy of a Corporate Takeover," in the *Ethics in America* series, in which a panel discusses a hypothetical takeover. A good case of an actual attempted takeover with an accompanying video is "Dayton Hudson: Conscience and Control."

6. The contractual theory can be explained in several ways. First, point out that many firms exist without shareholders; among these are sole proprietorships and partnerships and ask why large firms are usually not organized in these ways. Alternatively, ask why such firms would "go public," that is become a publicly held corporation with shareholders. These forms of organization encounter two related problems: (a) sole proprietors and partners assumes most of the risk, and (b) it is difficult to raise capital. Becoming a publicly held corporation solves both of these problems. Second, point out that corporations can be formed for any legal purpose. For example, a nonprofit corporation, such as the Red Cross, is also a nexus of contracts in which groups have come together for some purpose. Also, for-profit corporations can have some purpose beside making a profit; the New York Times is an example of a company that has the public service goal of providing news in its charter–and an ownership structure that safeguards this goal. Corporations can also be employee-owned (United Airlines), customer-owned (True Value Hardware is a supplier that is owned by the store owners who purchase from it), and supplier-owned (Ocean Spray is a growers cooperative). Ask why these kinds of firms exist. What contracting problems do they solve? And ask why other firms are organized as shareholder-owned firms?

7. The discussion of externalities on pages 354-55 refers to the Coase Theorem, which is cited in a footnote. The Coase Theorem asserts that externalities do not result in a misallocation of resources as long as there are no transaction costs and property rights are clearly assigned and enforceable. Instructors of students with an economics background might take time to explain and explore the Coase Theorem as a solution to the problem of externalities.

KEY TERMS AND CONCEPTS

A. P. Smith Manufacturing v. *Barlow*
affirmative duties
Caremark opinion
classical view (or corporate social responsibility)
code of ethics
contractual theory
Dodge v. *Ford Motor Co.*
equity/efficiency
ethics training
Federal Sentencing Guidelines
fiduciary (duty)
firm-specific assets
integrity and compliance strategies
Iron Law of Responsibility
managerial view
negative injunctions
nexus of contracts
philanthropy
property rights theory
residual risk
"rules of the game"
separation of ownership and control

social performance
social institution theory
social responsiveness
social responsibility
stakeholder (model)
taxation argument
transaction costs
trusteeship

CHAPTER FOURTEEN

ETHICS IN INTERNATIONAL BUSINESS

CHAPTER SUMMARY

This chapter deals with the ethical dilemmas of international business and, in particular, with the problem of different standards for business practice. Should a transnational corporation, which may operate in countries with different standards, follow the practices of the home country or those of the host country, or are there special ethical standards that apply in international business? The chapter examines these three possibilities and offers an ethical framework that includes the principle of negative harm and the principle of fundamental international rights.

CHAPTER OVERVIEW

Introduction

Although many firms engage in business abroad, most of the ethical issues in this area involve *transnational corporations* (TNCs), which are defined as firms that have a direct investment in two or more countries. This chapter is concerned primarily with the *moral* obligations of TNCs, especially in operations that affect less developed countries where standards are generally lower.

Developing an Ethical Framework

The crux of the charges against transnational corporations is that they adopt a double standard, doing in a host country what would be regarded as wrong if done at home. However, many of the criticized practices are legal and are even considered to be ethical in some less developed countries.

Two extreme positions might be expressed as "When in Rome, do as the Romans do" and "When in Rome or anywhere else, do as you would at home." Although the idea of eliminating double standards is admirable, such a high level of conduct is actually not morally required of TNCs in every instance for the following reasons.

1. The conditions prevailing in other parts of the world are different in some morally relevant respects from those in the United States and other developed countries.
2. American standards are not necessarily universal. Some aspects of U.S. law and practice reflect incidental features of our situation and do not express universal moral requirements.
3. The people in a host country have a right to decide on the standards to be applied.
4. Many factors in other countries, especially in the third world, are beyond the control of TNCs, and they often have little choice but to adapt to local conditions.

Special standards for international business.

The world of the TNC requires a slightly different approach to issues than the one appropriate to a corporation operating wholly within a single nation state. Some of the conditions that create a social responsibility for corporations in the U.S. are absent elsewhere. In addition, the lack of effective international law, with comprehensive multinational agreements and codes of conduct, creates a less regulated and more competitive environment for international business. Thus, TNCs do not have the same obligations abroad as they do at home.

Among the principles that might be part of an ethical framework for international business are the following:

1. *Minimal and maximal duties.* According to Thomas Donaldson, a *maximal duty* is one whose fulfillment would be "praiseworthy but not absolutely mandatory," whereas a *minimal duty* is one such that "the persistent failure to observe it would deprive the corporation of its moral right to exist." For example, a corporation's obligation to improve living conditions in a third world country would be a maximal duty, but every company has a minimal duty not to dump toxic wastes in populated areas. **2.** *Fundamental International Rights.* Fundamental international rights are roughly the same as natural and human rights, which are discussed in Chapter 3. The main problem with respecting the principle of fundamental international rights is that it is difficult to specify the rights in question. Donaldson stipulates that the right must protect something of very great value, must be subject to substantial and recurrent threats, and must satisfy a fairness-affordability test.
3. *The negative harm principle.* This principle holds that TNCs should not add substantially to the deprivation and suffering of people or expose them to great risk without their consent. The major problem with the negative harm principle is the difficulty in specifying the risk about which people have a right to be informed. Henry Shue proposes six criteria for the class of prohibited harms, according to which people have a right to be protected against the possibility of serious irreversible bodily damage that is undetectable, unpredictable, and likely to occur.
4. *The rational empathy test.* Donaldson proposes applying a principle of rational empathy, which involves putting ourselves in the shoes of the other persons and considering how the people affected would evaluate the benefits and harms. Rational empathy can be criticized in two ways. First, even limited empathy requires considerable knowledge of other cultures, and this might prove to be a psychological impossibility. Second, rational empathy offers no protection against the coercion that results from dire economic necessity.

Marketing Pharmaceuticals in the Third World

The pharmaceutical industry, more than any other industry, has been criticized for its activities abroad. These questionable practices include the use of different labels on products, drug dumping (the practice of selling abroad drugs that have not been approved for use domestically or for which approval has been withdrawn), different pricing, and bribery (which includes providing free samples that can be sold). TNCs are also able to avoid taxes and limits on the repatriation of profits by means of transfer pricing (the price that companies charge their own subsidiaries for goods). Advertising encourages the use of branded drugs instead of cheaper generics and prompts people to self-medicate and purchase useless pills.

Whether the marketing practices of pharmaceutical corporations involve a double standard is difficult to determine for many reasons, including different local conditions and different weighing of costs and benefits.

Foreign Bribery

The issue of foreign bribery is difficult for two reasons. First, the term *bribe* is vague, and there are many kinds of payments that must be distinguished from bribes. Second, the main ethical questions is not whether bribery is ethical (it's not) but whether paying a bribe is justified in a corrupt environment.

The definition of bribery in the Foreign Corrupt Practices Act (FCPA) has three elements: (a) what is offered, (b) the person to whom the offer is made, and (c) the purpose for which the offer is made. Each of these three elements involves many questions.

That bribery is wrong is supported by three main considerations: (a) the corruption of financial records that results when payments are not properly recorded in a company's records, (b) the impact of bribes on the political system of other countries and on American foreign policy, and (c) the disruption effect of bribes on fair and efficient markets.

The problem of foreign bribery has been addressed in the United States by the Foreign Corrupt Practices Act, which includes accounting requirements to ensure that all payments are correctly recorded and a provision that prohibits the use of agents where the the company "knows or has reason to know" that funds will be used to bribe foreign officials. Some critics charge that the FCPA places American companies at a competitive disadvantage and is a form of "ethical imperialism." Neither of these charges can be supported.

Among the agencies involved in efforts for combating foreign bribery are United Nations Commission on Transnationals, the World Bank, Transparency International, and the Organization for Economic Cooperation and Development. The members of the OECD have agreed to change their legal system to conform with the FCPA.

CASE SUMMARIES

14.1 The Tragedy at Bhopal

In 1984, an accidental explosion at a Union Carbide plant in Bhopal, India, released a lethal cloud of methyl isocyanate (MIC) that killed 3,500 people and injured at least 200,000. The explosion was the result of worker error, and damage from the explosion was compounded by multiple failures in the plant's backup emergency systems. The risk of an explosion was increased by cost-cutting measures that lowered safety standards and employed more dangerous technologies. Union Carbide built the plant at the urging of the Indian government because of the need for fertilizers and pesticides. The Indian government also encouraged the company to locate in Bhopal in order to promote development of the Madhya Pradesh region and insisted on manual safety systems in order to create more jobs. The number of deaths and injuries was increased by the buildup of shanties next to the plant that had been permitted by local authorities. In the aftermath, Union Carbide denied that it had any obligation to pay compensation, since it was only a 51 percent shareholder in Union Carbide India Limited. Ultimately, the company paid $470 million to compensate the victims of the accident. To date, few victims have received any money due to corruption by Indian officials, and Union Carbide was forced to lay off employees and sell its consumer products division.

Discussion Questions

1. Given the economic and political conditions under which it was operating in India, was Union Carbide morally justified in operating the plant as it did? The standard of safety was lower than the standard at Union Carbide plants in the United States. Is this an acceptable or an unacceptable double standard?
2. Union Carbide appears to have located and designed the plant in accord with the priorities of the Indian government and to have utilized a riskier process in order to produce a lower-cost pesticide. Are these reasonable trade-offs? What determines whether these are reasonable trade-offs?
3. Does Union Carbide have an obligation to compensate the victims of the accident? Does the fact that Union Carbide India Ltd. is a separate corporation in which Union Carbide owns 51 percent of the stock make any difference? Does the fact that the local government permitted residents to settle next to the plant make any difference?

Case Objectives

Unlike many cases that focus on the infliction of predictable harms, this case is concerned with the ethics of foreign operations that pose a certain level of (unpredictable) risk. Determining what constitutes an acceptable level of risk varies from one setting to another. Did India's desperate need to grow food for its increasing population override the risk of an industrial accident in a fertilizer and pesticide plant? The case also illustrates that sometimes negative consequences from TNC activities can be exacerbated by social, political, and economic conditions in the host country. The application of the negative harm and rational empathy tests yield inconclusive results. The accident caused great harm, but the benefits might have appeared to outweigh the risks. The lower safety standards might be justified by the Indian government's desire to provide jobs and boost agricultural production. The case also provides an opportunity to apply and test Henry Shue's criteria for prohibited harms.

Case 14.2 H. B. Fuller in Honduras

The H. B. Fuller Company, located in St. Paul, Minnesota, learned from press reports that one of the company's product, an adhesive called Resistol, was being sniffed by street children in Honduras with devastating consequences to their health. The company's reputation for socially responsible conduct was being questioned not only by activists and public health officials in Honduras but also by customers and shareholders in the United States. The Honduran government had addressed the problem by mandating that oil of mustard be added to Resistol to prevent its abuse, but company executives believed that this is not a satisfactory solution because oil of mustard produces some harmful side effects and also adversely affects the quality of the product. In addition, reformulation of the product does not appear to be feasible. Since the problems were caused by social conditions, the company also considered a community-based approach similar to that employed by Gillette when that company faced a similar situation in the United States. However, the conditions in Honduras are not suitable to such an approach.

Discussion Questions

1. **1.** Does H. B. Fuller have any responsibility for the abuse of Resistol by street children in Honduras? If Resistol were being abused by young people in the United States, would the responsibility of the company be any different?

2. Is the continued marketing of Resistol compatible with the company's statement of its social responsibility? How could the company respond to the angry letters from customers and shareholders?

3. Even though the addition of oil of mustard is not wholly satisfactory, should the company adopt this alternative? Is the company justified in not complying with the Honduran law requiring the addition of oil of mustard?

4. What other alternatives are available for addressing the problem of the abuse of Resistol? Should the company seek to work with the government? Are there other organizations with which the company could collaborate?

Case Objectives

This case illustrates the complexities of corporate social responsibility that are discussed in Chapter 13, as well as the challenges of international business described in this chapter. Whether H. B. Fuller has a responsibility to address the problem of the abuse of its product would be a difficult question if the abuse occurred in the United States, and the difficulty is compounded by the vastly different conditions that prevail in Honduras. As in the Campbell Soup case, the company is being forced by public pressure to address a problem for which company executives may believe they are not responsible; but unlike the Campbell Soup case, the problem is more difficult to address effectively. Withdrawing or reformulating the product would not reduce substance abuse of street children in Honduras but would ensure only that the company's product would not be involved. The only solution is to reduce substance abuse by street children in Honduras, and this lies beyond the power of H. B. Fuller to accomplish alone. In the United States, government and voluntary organizations can be enlisted as allies in a cooperative strategy, but such resources are largely lacking in Honduras. One lesson of the case is that the exercise of corporate social responsibility is facilitated by other institutions in society. H. B. Fuller has yet to satisfy critics of the company's handling of the problem, and so instructors may want to utilize news stories about the most recent developments.

Case 14.3 Shell Oil in Nigeria

In November 1995, when the Ogoni activist Ken Saro-Wiwa and six others were sentenced to death in what many considered to be an unfair trial, Shell Oil Company was called upon to intervene with the Nigerian government. The company refused on the grounds that it would be inappropriate for a private company to interfere in the affairs of a sovereign state and that interfering would only "inflame the issues." Critics pointed out that Shell Oil was already deeply implicated in Nigerian affairs inasmuch as oil earnings totaling $10 billion annually provided 80 percent of all government revenues. After attacks on Shell Oil facilities, the company accepted police protection and provided arms to the local police, and, according to critics, Shell also provided transportation and participated in planning. Much of the controversy centered on the area known as Ogoniland, where oil production produced a great amount of pollution but few benefits for the people. Ken Saro-Wiwa was a leader of the Movement for the Survival of the Ogoni People (MOSOP), who was accused of instigating the murder of several Ogoni chiefs in a dispute over tactics for MOSOP. Violence in Ogoniland had led Shell Oil to withdraw from the region in January of 1993. In response to the company's withdrawal, the Nigerian government had undertaken security operations in order to induce Shell to return.

Discussion Questions

1. Is Shell's position on noninterference in the affairs of a sovereign government justified? How could company executives respond to critics? Note that Shell's position is considered to be morally required and that many companies have been criticized for excessive involvement.

2. What else could or should Shell have done to protect its property and personnel against attacks? Would the company have been justified in not cooperating with local security forces?

3. Did Shell Oil contribute to the underlying problem? What could or should the company have done differently in the events leading up to the civil unrest in Ogoniland? In particular, was Shell's environmental record a contributing factors?

4. What factors, other than Shell's conduct, led to the crisis? Are all petroleum companies vulnerable to the kind of problems Shell faced? If so, what factors make petroleum companies vulnerable? Were some factors out of Shell's control? In particular, did the corruption and ruthlessness of the Nigerian government play a role? If so, how can any company act responsibly in such an environment?

5. What should Shell Oil do after the execution of Ken Saro-Wiwa? Should the company make a partial or full withdrawal from Nigeria, or resume operation in Ogoniland, or even expand operations?

Case Objectives

"Shell Oil in Nigeria" helps students explore issues about the involvement of transnational corporations in the domestic affairs of host countries, especially when these countries have repressive and corrupt governments. Some companies (such as ITT in Chile) have been charged with excessive interference, and others (such as U.S. companies involved in South Africa during the period of apartheid) saw their choices as staying or withdrawing without getting involved in politics. In some situations, however, companies may have no choice but to become involved. What principles should guide companies in such situations? It may be argued that Shell Oil contributed to the problem by failing to protect the environment and working with the local people to improve conditions. Could such activities have been undertaken without interfering in Nigeria's domestic affairs? Finally, the case illustrates the problem of operating in a repressive and corrupt environment. To what extent does a company's involvement with a corrupt dictatorship amount to complicity?

TEACHING STRATEGIES

1. In teaching about international business ethics, it is important for students to understand the realities of global business. Ask students to research U.S. companies that manufacturer products in less-developed countries and to find sources that describe workers' wages and working conditions and government labor laws in these countries. In recent years, U.S. apparel companies, including the Gap and Nike, have been criticized for their relations with contractors in Asia. Many of these companies have cooperated in developing the Workplace Code of Conduct." Many videos depict conditions in graphic terms. Two very powerful, but dated, documentaries are "Controlling Interest: The World of the Multinational Corporation" and "Hungry for Profit." More recent is "Globalization and Human Rights." The ethical criticism of pharmaceutical marketing practices, which is discussed in the textbook, is further illustrated in "For Export Only: Pharmaceuticals." Also, the case on Green Giant (Case 4.1) and the video "Your Job or Mine?" (which is described in chapter 4 of this manual) can be used in the context of international business ethics.

2. Foreign bribery and especially the Foreign Corrupt Practices Act provide good subjects for discussion. The case "Lockheed in Japan" (Case 2.1) can be recalled and discussed in the context of international business. "Wait International and Questionable Payments" in *Cases in Ethics and the Conduct of Business* focuses on the development of a corporate policy in response to the 1988 revisions of the Foreign Corrupt Practices Act. An effective case involving an executive who must decide whether to submit to a bribery demand is "The Project at Moza Island," in Thomas Donaldson and Al Gini, eds., *Case Studies in Business Ethics*, 4th ed. (Prentice Hall, 1996).

3. The question of the extraterritorial application of U.S. law is raised not only in the Foreign Corrupt Practices Act but also in many other laws. In particular, the application of Title VII of the 1964 Civil Rights Act to employees of American firms abroad is a good topic for discussion. A widely-used case on possible sexual discrimination in the Mexican office of a U.S. bank is "Foreign Assignment," in Donaldson and Gini, eds., *Case Studies in Business Ethics*, 4th ed. A useful discussion is Don Mayer and Anita Cava, "Ethics and the Gender Equality Dilemma for U.S. Multinationals," *Journal of Business Ethics*, 12 (1993), 701-708.

4. Some instructors might want to examine views of business ethics by business people in other countries. Unfortunately, the literature on this topic is scarce. For a general comparison of U.S., European, and Japanese views, see David Vogel, "The Globalization of Business Ethics: Why America Remains Distinctive," *California Management Review*, 35 (Fall 1992), 30-49. Japanese views of business ethics are explained and explored in two helpful articles: Iwao Taka, "Business Ethics: A Japanese View," *Business Ethics Quarterly*, 4 (1994), 53-78; and Ernest Gundling, "Ethics and Working with the Japanese: The Entrepreneur and the 'Elite Course'," *California Management Review*, 33 (Spring 1991), 25-39. For Russia and China, see Sheila M. Puffer and Daniel J. McCarthy, "Finding the Common Ground in Russian and American Business Ethics," *California Management Review*, 37 (Winter 1995), 29-46; and Lu Xiaohe, "Business Ethics in China," *Journal of Business Ethics*, 16 (1997), 1509-1518.

5. International business is ethically problematical because of a lack of background institutions and a well-developed system of international law. This void is being filled by a number of codes of conduct for transnational corporations, which can be profitably examined in a classroom discussion. In particular, the Caux Round Table "Principles for Business" and the "Principles for Global Corporate Responsibility," developed by a consortium of religious organizations, provide good examples of international codes of conduct. See also the OECD "Guidelines for Multinational Enterprises" at www.oecd.org. A good discussion of the ethical force of such codes is William E.

Frederick, "The Moral Authority of Transnational Codes of Corporate Ethics," *Journal of Business Ethics*, 10 (March 1991), 165-177.

6. A practical problem for corporations with codes of ethics and ethics programs in adapting these for global business. See Kevin T. Jackson, "Globalizing Corporate Ethics Programs," *Journal of Business Ethics*, 16 (1997), 1227-1235. It may be useful to return to any actual codes of ethics that students examined in the context of the discussion of ethics programs in Chapter 13 and focus on their applicability for international business.

7. A source of ethical issues that is not discussed in the textbook is the transition from socialism to capitalism in the former Soviet Union and Central and Eastern Europe. For a summary of these problems, see Jacques Attali, "The Ethics of European Transition," *Business Ethics: A European Review*, 2 (1993), 111-116.

KEY WORDS

bribery
direct investment
double standard
drug dumping
ethical imperialism
facilitating ("grease") payment
fairness-affordability criterion
Foreign Corrupt Practices Act
fundamental international rights
home/host country
maximal/minimal duty
morally relevant difference
negative harm principle
principle of negative harm
prohibited harms
rational empathy test
trade-offs
transfer pricing
transnational corporation

APPENDIX

A NOTE ON SOURCES

The sources in business ethics are immense and growing rapidly, and so this note can serve only to point an instructor in the right direction. The best advice is, get connected! There are many ways to receive relevant and timely information, but the first step is to become involved in the field of business ethics.

The primary source of information about books and journals, upcoming events, videos, and Internet resources is *The Society for Business Ethics Newsletter*, which is published quarterly. The newsletter may be received by becoming a member of the Society for Business Ethics, which is the major organization of business ethics scholars. For information about the Society for Business Ethics, consult the Society's web site at: www.luc.edu/depts/business/sbe. Membership in the Society also includes a subscription to the Society's journal, *Business Ethics Quarterly*. Membership dues are $50 ($55 for person outside the United States and Canada); please make checks payable to "Society for Business Ethics." To join the Society for Business Ethics, send your name, address, and institutional affiliation, along with a check for to:

Society for Business Ethics
c/o Laura Charland
Philosophy Documentation Center
Bowling Green State University
Bowling Green, OH 43403-0189

The principal journals in business ethics are: *Business Ethics Quarterly*, which is the journal of the Society for Business Ethics, and *Journal of Business Ethics*. The journal, *Teaching Business Ethics*, is devoted to the publication of articles on pedagogy. See copies of these journals for subscription information.

Important reference sources for teaching business ethics is *The Blackwell Encyclopedic Dictionary of Business Ethics*, edited by R. Edward Freeman and Patricia H. Werhane, which contains more than 350 entries written by the leading experts in the field of business ethics, and *A Companion to Business Ethics*, edited by Robert E. Frederick, which contains essays on areas of business ethics by leading experts in the field..

Ethics and the Conduct of Business, 3rd ed., contains 47 short cases for classroom discussion. For longer, "business school-type" cases, consult the accompanying casebook, John R. Boatright, ed., *Cases in Ethics and the Conduct of Business*, also published by Prentice Hall. Another casebook is Thomas Donaldson and Al Gini, eds., *Case Studies in Business Ethics*, 4th ed. (Prentice Hall, 1996). Two sources for individual cases, some of which are listed in this instructor's manual, are the Harvard Business School at www.hbsp.harvard.edu and the Darden School of the University of Virginia at www.darden.viginia.edu. Each school maintains a web site that contains a complete catalog of cases along with instructions for ordering cases. The Business Enterprise Trust develops cases that recognize "acts of business leadership which combine sound management and social conscience." These cases and accompanying videos are now available from Harvard Business School Publishing. Arthur Andersen & Co. developed a set of long cases and another set of short scenarios as part of a five-year business ethics program conducted between 1987 and 1992. These cases are no longer available from Arthur Andersen & Co., but they might still be found through the network of campus coordinators that was established as part of the program.

Many videos are available for classroom use, and, properly used, they make a very valuable supplement to the textbook and cases. Because videos are available from many sources, no sources are listed for the videos that are recommended in this manual. Instructors are advised to consult the comprehensive catalogs that are generally available in university libraries. Your institution may already own some of the recommended videos, and others can be obtained by means of interlibrary loan or purchased or rented from a distributor. A survey of some relevant videos released before 1989 is provided in LaRue Tone Hosmer, "Teaching Business Ethics: The Use of Films and Videotapes," *Journal of Business Ethics*, 8 (1989), 929-936. An excellent series of video vignettes has been developed by the Ethics Resource Center, 1747 Pennsylvania Avenue, NW, Suite 400, Washington, DC 20006, telephone (202) 737-2258. The web site for The Ethics Resource Center is www.ethics.org.

A final source of material is the daily newspaper and the business press. Some instructors ask students to gather and present stories on business ethics as part of the discussion in every class period. The opportunity to link the text material and cases to unfolding events greatly enriches the teaching of business ethics.